CHILDREN'S ENCYCLOPEDIA

THE WORLD OF KNOWLEDGE

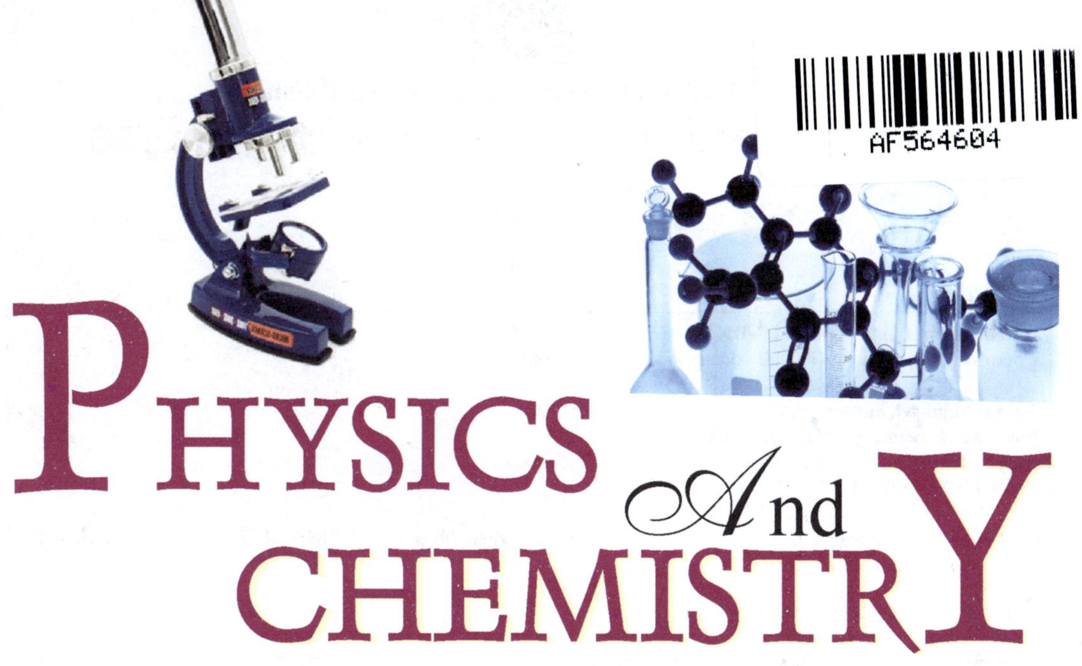

PHYSICS And CHEMISTRY

by

Manasvi Vohra

V&S PUBLISHERS

Published by:

Head Office
F-2/16, Ansari Road, Daryaganj,
New Delhi-110002 ☎23240026, 27
✉ info@vspublishers.com
🌐 www.vspublishers.com

Regional Office
5-1-707/1, Brij Bhawan (Beside Central Bank of India Lane) Bank Street, Koti,
Hyderabad - 500 095 ☎ 040-24737290
✉ vspublishershyd@gmail.com

Online Brandstore: amazon.in/vspublishers

Buy Books Online: amazon • Flipkart | **Follow us on:**    

ISBN 978-93-505703-7-1

New Edition

Cataloging in Publication Data--DK
Courtesy: D.K. Agencies (P) Ltd. <docinfo@dkagencies.com>

Vohra, Manasvi, author.
Physics and chemistry / Manasvi Vohra.
pages cm. -- (Children's encyclopedia : the world of knowledge)
ISBN 9789350570371

1. Physics--Encyclopedias, Juvenile. 2. Chemistry--Encyclopedias, Juvenile. I. Title. II. Series: Children's encyclopedia : the world of knowledge.

LCC QC25.V64 2024 | DDC 530.03 23

Printed at : Param Offsetters, Okhla, New Delhi–110020

PUBLISHER'S NOTE

V&S Publishers is glad to announce the launch of a unique, fully *coloured set of five books* under the head, ***Children's Encyclopedia – The World of Knowledge.*** The set of 5 books namely – ***Life Sciences and the Human Body***, ***Physics and Chemistry***, ***Space Science and Electronics***, ***Scientists and Inventions*** and ***General Knowledge*** has been especially developed keeping in mind the students and children of all age groups, particularly from 6 to 14 years of age. Our main aim is to arouse the interest and solve the queries of the school children regarding the various and diverse topics of Science and help them master the subject thoroughly. After the resounding success of 71 Science Trailblazing Series, we present you with this new arrival of ours.

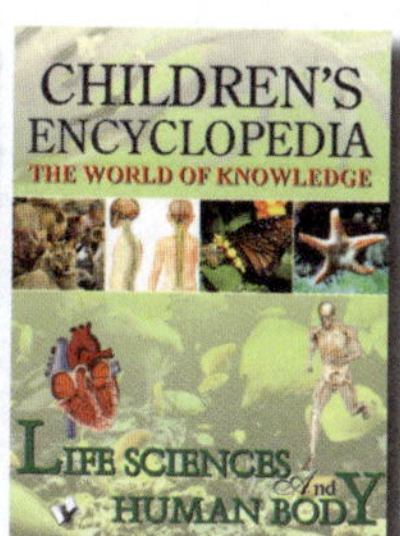

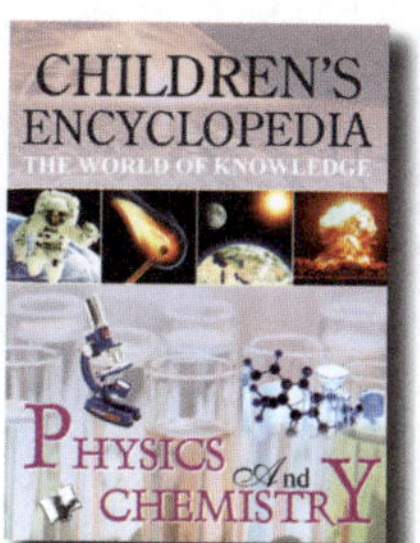

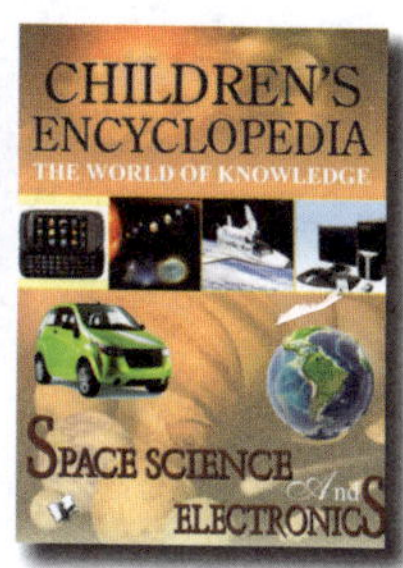

In the book, ***Physics and Chemistry,*** the author has broadly dealt with some interesting and fascinating Scientific facts in the first part (Part-I) like *Energy, Electrical Energy, Magnetism, Energy Waves, Light, Sound, Heat, Force, Motion,* etc. The second part (Part-II), on the other hand, focusses mainly on *Matter, Properties of Matter, Changing States of Matter, Mass, Volume and Density, Atoms, Molecules, Elements, Properties of Elements, Chemical Reactions and Changes, Acids and Bases* and so on.....

Each chapter is followed by a section called **Quick Facts** that contains a set of interesting and fascinating facts about the topics already discussed in the chapter. There are also **Exercises** compiled at the end of the book followed by a **Glossary** of difficult words and scientific terms to make the book complete and comprehensive.

Though our aim is to be flawless, but errors might have crept in inadvertently. So we request our esteemed readers to read the book thoroughly and offer valuable suggestions wherever necessary to improve and enhance the quality of the book. Hope it interests you all and serves its purpose well.

CONTENTS

PHYSICS

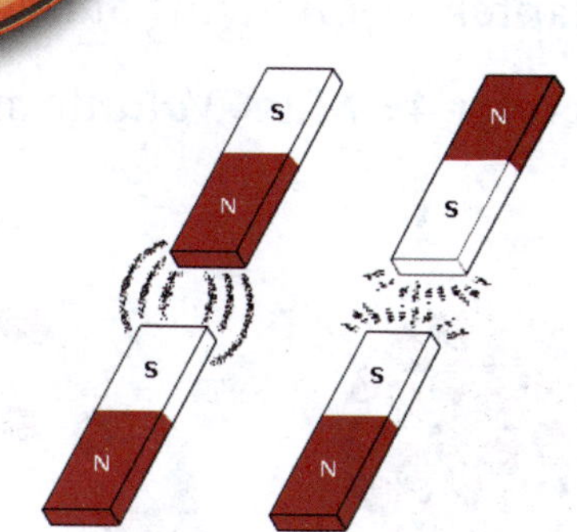

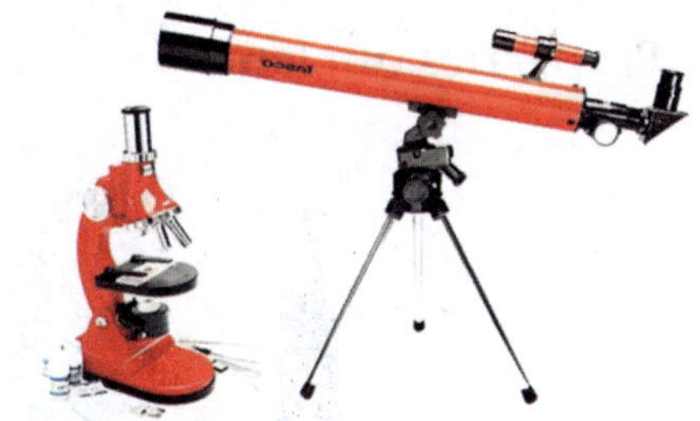

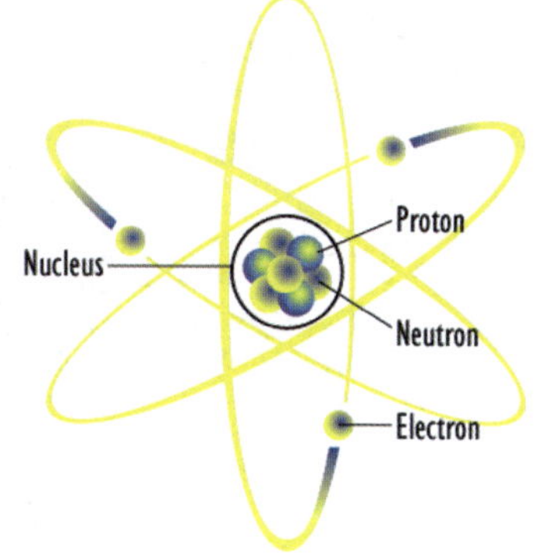

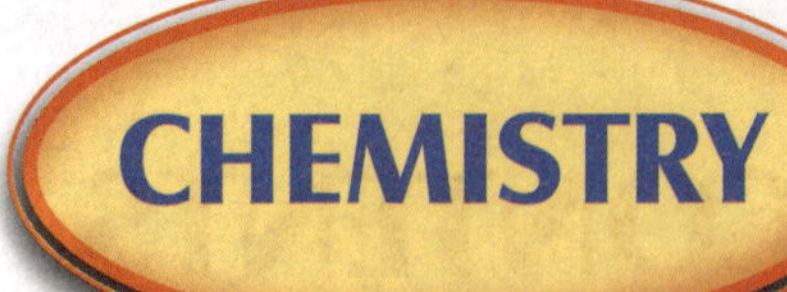

CHEMISTRY

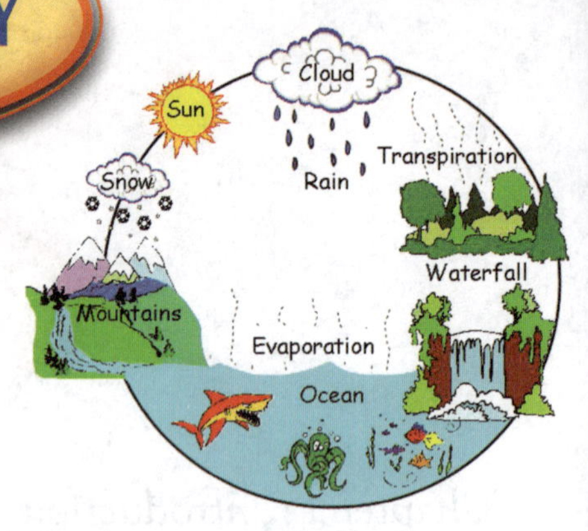
Cloud
Sun
Snow
Rain
Transpiration
Waterfall
Mountains
Evaporation
Ocean

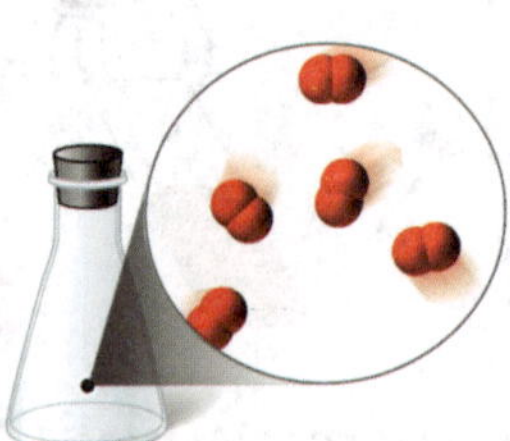

CHANGE
RAIN
FAIR
STORMY
VERY DRY
BAROMETER

PHYSICS

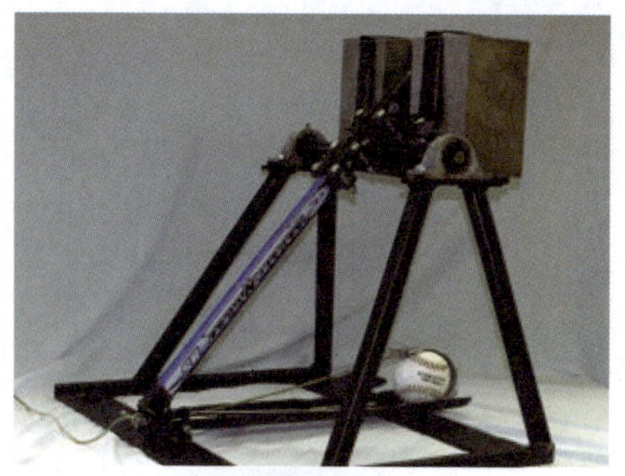

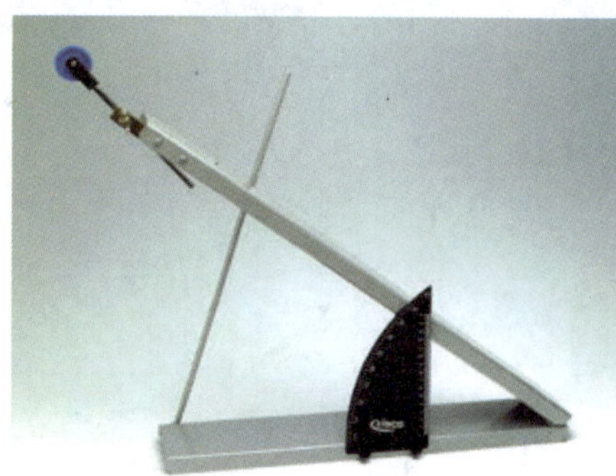

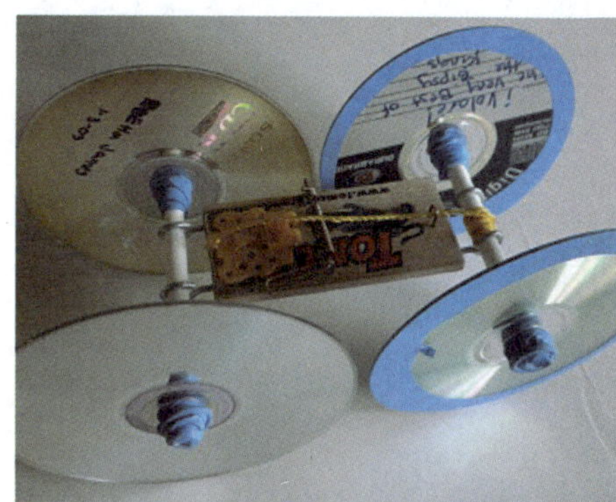

Chapter - 1

INTRODUCTION

What is Physics?

Physics is a natural *science that helps us to study forces and their impact on the environment*. Physics helps us to understand how our universe behaves. It is the study of **matter** and **energy** in **space** and **time** and how they are related to each other. In other words, it is the general analysis of nature. Physics is a quantitative science because it uses numbers for measurement. A scientist who researches in Physics is called a **physicist**.

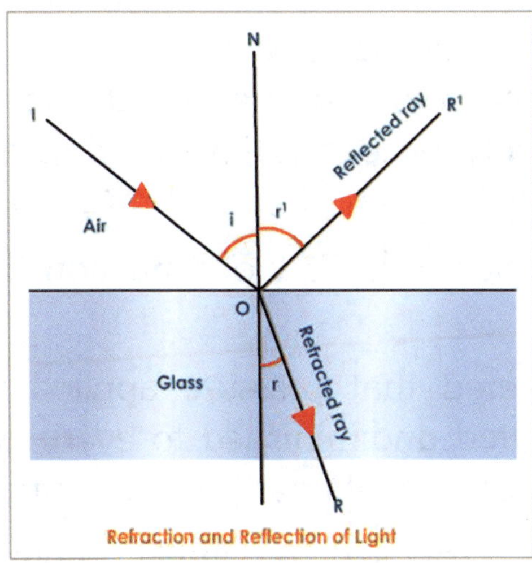

Reflection & Refraction of Light

Experiments with Magnet

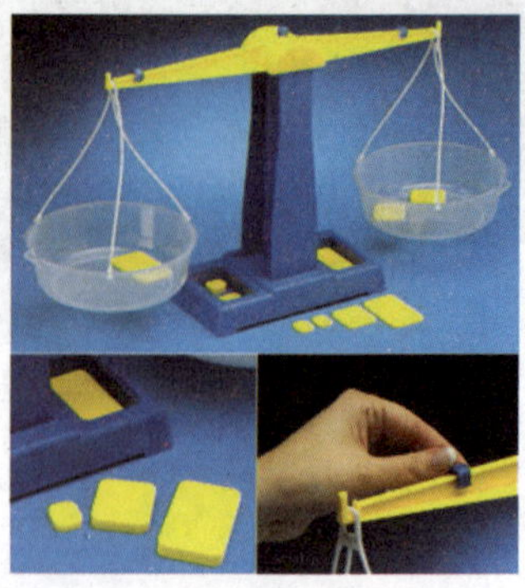

Weight Experiment

Some popular physicists and their contributions:

- **William Gilbert:** Hypothesized that the earth is a giant magnet
- **Sir Isaac Newton:** 1643–1727 Developed theories of gravitation and mechanics
- **Benjamin Franklin:** 1706–1790 Characterised two kinds of electric charges – positive and negative
- **James Watt:** 1736–1819 Invented the modern steam engine.
- **Count Alessandro Volta:** 1745–1827 Pioneered in the study of electricity
- **Aristotle:** Golden Mean, Reason, Logic, Syllogism – Besides these important topics, he also discussed on the topics of matter, change, movement, space, position and time as well as studied comets.
- **Willebrod Snell:** Discovered the law of refraction (Snell's law)
- **Blaise Pascal:** Discovered that pressure applied to an enclosed fluid is transmitted undiminished to every part of the fluid and to the walls of its container (Pascal's principle)
- **Christiaan Huygens:** Proposed a simple geometrical

wave theory of light, now known as "Huygen's principle"; pioneered the use of pendulum in clocks

- **Robert Hooke:** Discovered Hooke's law of elasticity
- **Sir Albert Einstein:** Explained Brownian motion and photoelectric effect; contributed to the theory of atomic spectra; formulated theories of special and general relativity
- **Benjamin Franklin:** The first American physicist; characterised two kinds of electric charge, which he named 'positive' and 'negative'
- **Lord Kelvin:** Proposed absolute temperature scale, also developed the essence to the development of thermodynamics
- **Michael Faraday:** Discovered electromagnetic induction and devised the first electrical transformer
- **George Ohm:** Discovered that the flow of current is proportional to potential difference and inversely proportional to resistance (Ohm's law)
- **Andre Marie Ampere:** Father of electrodynamics

Chapter - 2

ENERGY

Energy makes everything happen. It helps us to do things. We need energy to move, grow and think. We need energy to run our vehicles. Animals and plants also need energy to survive. It is the power to change things and to do work. The total energy contained in an object is defined by its mass.

Solar Thermal Energy

Types of Energy

1. Stored Energy

Stored energy is the energy that is used later. An object can be made to store energy and use it later when required. We as humans also store energy in our bodies and use it when needed. In objects like a clockwork toy, energy is stored in the spring. When the spring is released, the toy starts working. Stored energy is also called **Potential Energy** because it has the potential to make things work.

Potential Energy

Movement Energy

When a car moves downhill, the height gives it potential energy. As the car moves downward, the potential energy turns into movement energy and makes the car go faster This is also called the **Kinetic Energy**.

Nuclear Energy

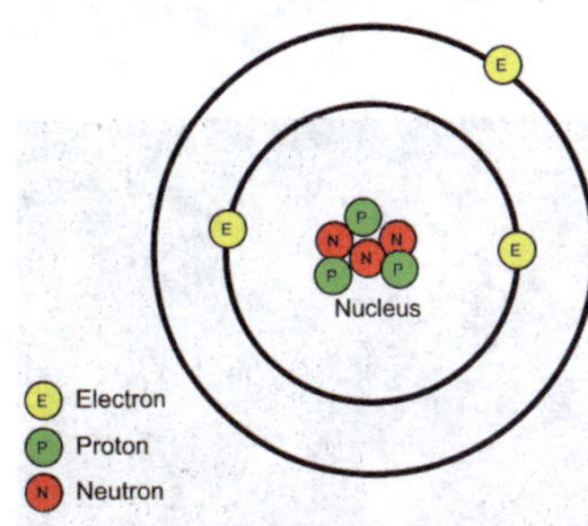

Any matter is made up of several small particles called **atoms**. At the centre of the atom is a **nucleus** which stores a huge amount of energy. This **nuclear energy** is used in power stations to produce **electricity**.

Quick Facts

- Energy can neither be created nor destroyed by itself. It can only be transformed.
- There is as much energy in this world as there was billions of years ago.
- Energy only changes form. For example: When we burn wood, we change its energy into heat and light. This is also called the Law of Conservation of Energy.

Chapter - 3

ELECTRICAL ENERGY

Electrical energy exists in the natural world in **storm clouds**. This energy turns into **lightning** that gives **heat** and **light** and **thunder** which gives **sound**.

Lighting and Thunder

Energy Conversion

Dam (Hydel Power)

One form of energy can be easily converted into another with the help of a device, for example a battery, where *chemical energy* is turned into *electrical energy*, and a dam, where **potential energy** is turned into **electrical energy**.

Coal Contains Chemical Energy

Boiling water creates steam. Moving steam has **kinetic energy** which moves turbines.

Burning coal provides heat energy which is used to boil water.

Kinetic energy produced by moving turbines creates **electricity**.

Electrical energy used by television sets changes into **light**, **sound** and **heat energy**.

The Sun

Sun

The sun is the main source of energy on the earth. We get almost all our energy from the sun. Plants store the sun's energy as **chemical energy**. When we eat these plants, the energy enters our body as food and is released inside our body cells. All the animals and plants obtain energy from the sun in this way.

Since earlier times, humans have harnessed the sun's energy for use. The sun's energy reaches us primarily in the form of **radiation**. All the renewable sources derive their energy from the sun.

The sun's energy warms the planet, which results in differences in heat and pressure that change the weather patterns and ocean currents. It is because of the sun's energy that we have different seasons. The energy of the sun makes life possible on the earth.

Electrical Charge

In our homes, there are numerous appliances that work from electricity. Our television sets, computers, microwaves and the lights and fans — all use electricity to work. To make these appliances work, you need the flow of electricity.

Electricity can be produced by various different methods.

1. Thermal Power Plants: In thermal power plants, electricity is produced by steam. The water is heated and steam is produced. The steam turns a turbine which is connected to an electrical generator.

Thermal Power Plant

Hydro Power Plant

2. Hydro Power Plants: In hydro power plants, electricity is produced by harnessing the power of running water. The kinetic power of moving or falling water turns the turbines which in turn are connected to an electrical generator.

Wind Turbines

3. Wind Turbines: Wind mills harness the power of the wind and produce electricity. A wind turbine converts the kinetic energy of wind into mechanical energy. This mechanical energy is then used to produce electricity.

Solar Power

4. Solar Power: By capturing the power of the sun, electricity can be produced. The solar power is converted into electricity. Solar power needs to be stored also because sunlight is not available at night.

Nuclear Power Plant

5. Nuclear Power Plants: Nuclear power plants use nuclear power reactors to produce electricity. The heat from the reactors is used to generate steam which drives the turbines connected to generators to produce electricity.

There are two types of electric currents.

Static Electricity: It refers to the electric charge of an object. It is the build up of charge on the surface of an object.

A bolt of lightning is a huge spark of static electricity in the sky.

Electric Current: It refers to the flow of electric charge through an object. Electric current can be delivered through wires as a power source. This charge needs a good conductor if the transfer of electricity is to be done. The unit for measuring the rate of flow of electric charge is **ampere**. Electric charge is measured using an **ammeter**.

Electrification by Friction: Rub a balloon to your hair for five minutes and then take it near a wall. It sticks to the wall because it is now electrically charged because of the friction that was between the balloon and your hair.

Use of electricity in everyday lives:

For Heating: Heating up of home appliances like iron and geysers.

For Lighting: Lighting up our houses with the use of light bulbs.

For Communication: Powering telephones and computers.

For Transport: Electricity powers electric bikes and cars.

Quick Facts

- The electric energy or electricity is the potential energy associated with the conservative Coulomb forces between charged particles contained within a system, where the reference potential energy is usually chosen to be zero for particles at infinite separation.
- The movement of electric charge is known as an electric current, and its intensity is usually measured in amperes. Current can consist of any moving charged particles, most commonly these are electrons, but any charge in motion constitutes a current.

- **The sources of energy we use to make electricity can be renewable or non-renewable, but electricity itself is neither renewable or non-renewable.**
- **The cost of electricity is going up (both in dollars and in environmental and health impacts) and it doesn't show any signs of doing otherwise. About half of the energy in the American grid is coal generated.**

Chapter - 4

MAGNETISM

A magnetic field is created by moving electrical charges. Magnets have a north pole and a south pole. A magnetic field is defined by lines of force that go from the north pole to the south pole.

Magnets contain iron or a similar metal and exert a force called magnetism which attracts other objects with iron in them.

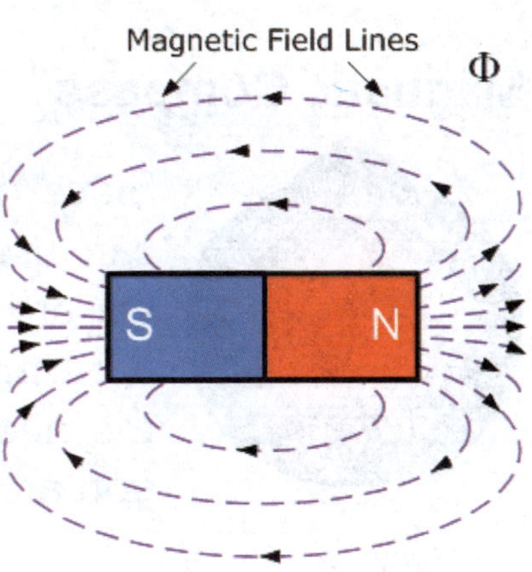

A Magnetic Field

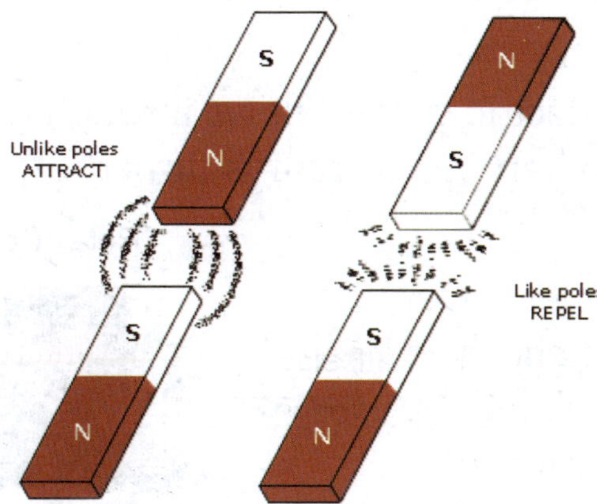

Unlike Poles Attract and Like Poles Repel

The force is called **attraction** when the materials are pulled together.

The force is called **repulsion** when the materials push apart.

Opposite poles *attract* each other while similar poles *repel* each other.

Northern Lights

The Earth has a huge magnetic field. The lights caused when particles from the solar wind are sucked into the Earth's magnetic field are called northern lights. Northern lights are also called *Aurora Borealis*. These lights can be seen in the northern hemisphere near the North Pole on a clear night.

Northern Lights

Magnetic Compass

Since our Earth has a huge magnetic field, we can use a magnet to find the direction, where we are moving. Four directions are marked on a **compass** – *north, south, east and west*. When the needle of the compass points to 'N' means you are travelling in the north direction.

Electromagnets

An electromagnet is made when an electric current flows through a **coil** and makes the coil magnetic. When the current is turned off, the magnetic field disappears.

An advantage of an electromagnet over permanent magnet is that the magnetic field of an electromagnet can be manipulated by controlling the amount of electric current. Also a continuous supply of energy is required to maintain the magnetic field.

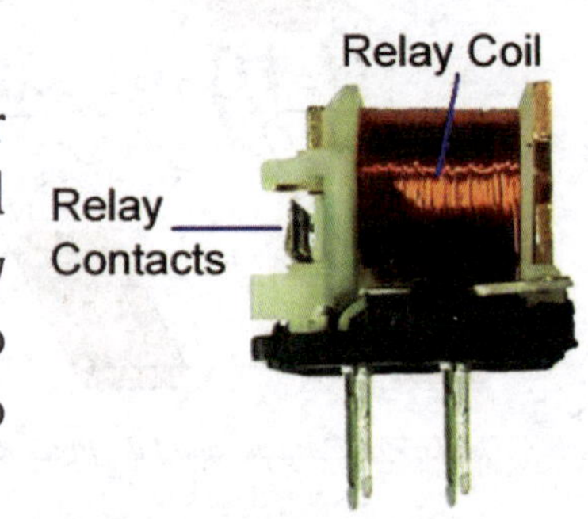

A Coil of Wire Wrapped around An Iron Core

Electromagnets are widely used in motors, electric bells, loudspeakers, MRI machines, industrial lifting magnets, etc. The device that measures the strength of a magnetic field is called a **magnetometer**.

Lifting Magnets

Lifting magnets are used in many places. They are used to search for metal objects in places that are difficult to reach by humans like land mines in a war zone. Lifting magnets can separate metal particles from oil or water.

The most important use of a lifting magnet can be in a junkyard. The magnet can find all the metal particles within trash. These metals can then be recycled and reused. Lifting magnets are also used by cranes for lifting very heavy metal cargo.

Magnetic Rails

Also known as *Maglev* or *Magnetic Levitation* uses a magnetic force to hold the trains above the tracks. These trains travel on air as there is a gap between the train and the rail. Magnets are used to create both lift and thrust for the trains. Such trains move fast and more smoothly and quietly than any other.

The wear and tear in such trains is very less and therefore, they work for a much longer time than trains that run on wheels. The acceleration and breaking is also faster.

China's Magnetic Rail

The first commercial Maglev was opened in *Birmingham, England* in 1984. The system was closed in 1995 due to reliability problems. The highest speed record of a *Maglev is 581km/hr* achieved by *Japan in 2003*.

Quick Facts

- The earth is a giant magnet and its magnetic field is like a bar magnet at the centre.
- A magnet is usually made of iron or steel-iron, nickel, cobalt, etc.
- A magnetic pull is strongest at two points–north and south poles.
- The first magnets were stones called Lodestones. The word, lode means lead. The stone magnetised compass needles and helped bring sailors home.
- Some vets use magnets to retrieve wire and metal from animals' stomachs.
- There are different types of magnets: permanent/ hard, temporary/soft, and electromagnets.
- The compass was used hundreds of years ago by Chinese sailors.
- Superconductors are the strongest magnets-made from coils of wire.

Chapter - 5

ENERGY WAVES

Energy travels in waves. A wave is a disturbance that travels through space and time and transfers energy. Like when you throw a small pebble in a lake, the waves will be small and close together and if the size of the pebble is large, then the waves will be larger and further apart.

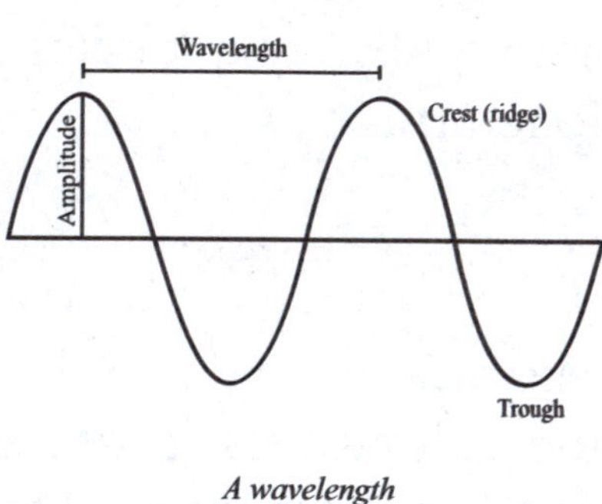

A wavelength

The Spectrum

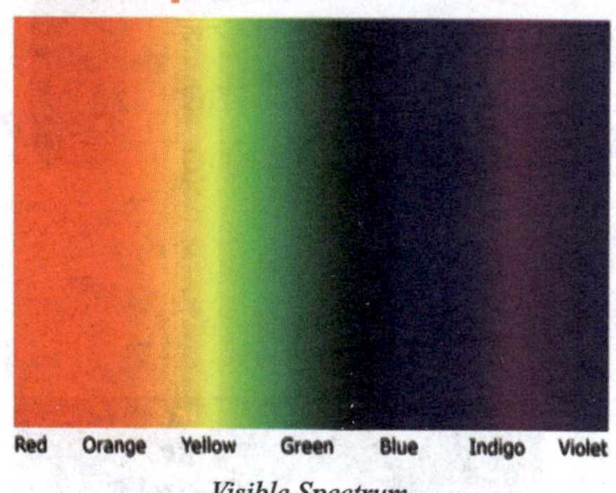

Visible Spectrum

The spectrum is an arrangement according to visible, ultraviolet and infrared light. Light is a type of energy wave that we can see. But there are also waves at different wavelengths that we cannot see. Some have larger wavelengths and some have smaller wavelengths.

Points to Remember

The distance between the peaks of two waves is called the **wavelength**.

There are **seven different waves** in our **light spectrum**:

1. Radio Waves

Radio waves have the longest wavelength and travel far. Man-made radio waves are used for a variety of purposes. These waves are used to send or receive information or to see. Radio and television use radio waves to send and receive information. These instruments can get information with the help of an antenna.

A **radar** is an instrument which detects rays reflected by objects and then shows the object on a **screen**. The distance of the object can also be calculated by seeing how long it takes for the waves to return.

2. Microwaves

Microwaves have a lesser wavelength than the radio waves. These are used in *microwave ovens* to heat food. Microwaves are also used in fibre optic cables to make long distance telephone calls. *Wireless* and *Bluetooth* also use microwaves. Another important use of microwaves is in the Global Navigation Satellite System and Global Positioning System.

3. Infrared Waves

Infrared waves include most of the thermal radiation emitted by objects near room temperature. Infrared is used in various industrial, scientific and medical purposes. An *infrared camera* can detect infrared waves to create images. Most of the energy from the sun received by the earth is also in the form of *infrared radiation*.

4.Visible Light

Visible light is the electromagnetic waves that we can see. Light waves bounce off the objects around us which makes it possible to see things. Visible light includes all the colours of the rainbow and each colour also has a different wavelength.

Do it Yourself

Take a **prism** and a **white sheet of paper**. Hold the prism on the paper and let sunlight fall through the prism. You will be able to see all the colours of the rainbow.

A Prism

Ultraviolet or UV rays have a wavelength smaller than that of visible light. UV rays are invisible to humans, but a number of insects can see the UV rays. Humans can see the effects of UV rays as **sunburn**. If you spend a long time in the sun, you get a **tan**. This tan is caused by the UV rays. Long exposure to the UV rays can cause *cancer* and *eye damage*.

5. X-rays

X-rays can penetrate solid objects and are used to take *images of the inside of objects*. The most common use of x-rays is taking photographs of the skeletal system. The x-rays penetrate our skin but not the bones. Therefore, an x-ray can very clearly show our bones.

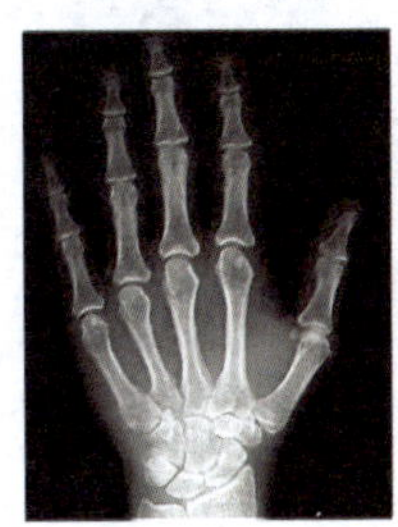

6. Gamma Rays

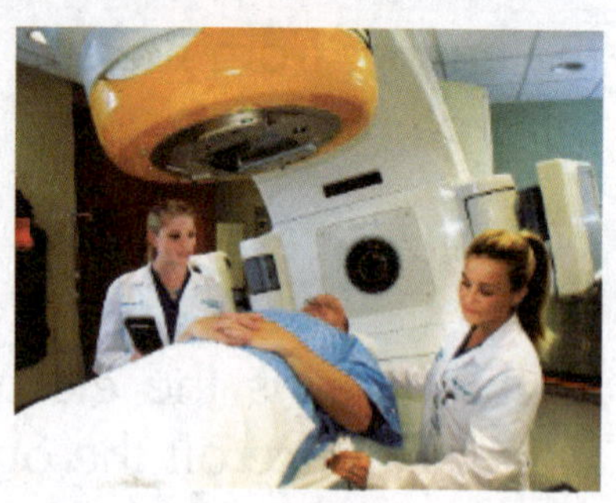

Gamma rays have the *shortest wavelengths*. The wavelength of a gamma ray can be as small as the nucleus of an atom. These are the most deadly because they are packed with energy. Gamma rays can break the DNA molecules, therefore they are used to *kill cancer cells*.

Quick Facts

- **Ultraviolet simply means "beyond light". In this case, the visible type that we, humans can see. It is also called "black light" due to it being invisible.**
- **UV rays can be used to sterilise and disinfect hospital and other medical equipments. This happens when the equipment in question is exposed to artificial light created by the UV lamps. The Ultraviolet radiation emitted by the lamps kills any living cells (good or bad) on the equipment.**

Chapter - 6

LIGHT

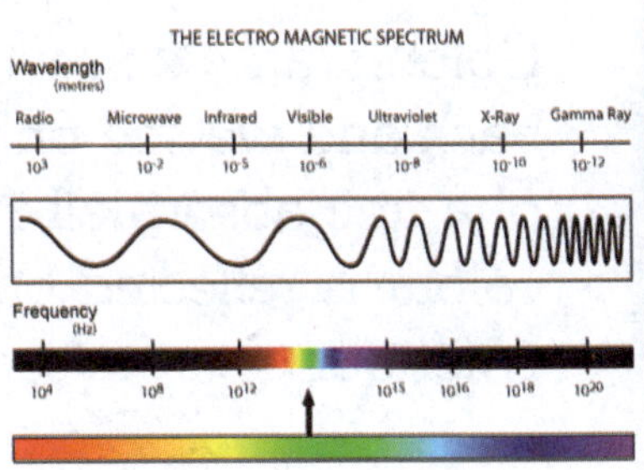

The Electro Magnetic Spectrum

Light or visible light is the **electromagnetic radiation** that we can see. It is because of light that we can see. Light contains all the colours mixed together and therefore, we see light as *white*. We receive all the natural light from the sun. Humans have made artificial light too which help us see in the dark. Light only travels in straight lines. If light is blocked by a solid object, *shadows* are cast.

Reflection of Light

Reflection of Light

When the rays of light fall on a surface and it is bounced back, it is called **reflection of light**. For example, when light falls on a glass and is reflected back, we can see our own image in it, which is called a **mirror**.

Refraction of Light

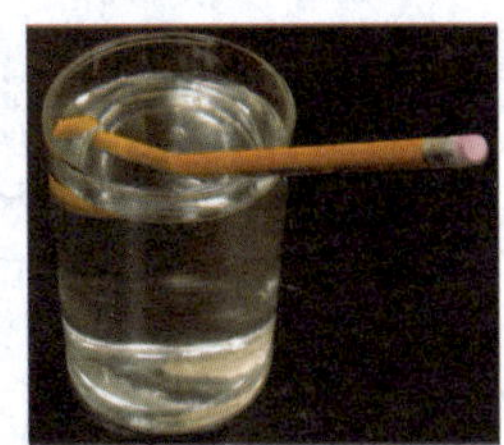

Refraction is the *bending of a light wave* when it travels from *one medium to the other*. The refraction takes place because the speed of light is different in different mediums.

Absorption of Light

Some objects absorb light. As all the colours in light have different wavelengths, it happens that some colours are absorbed and some are reflected back. When an object absorbs all the light, it is seen as **black**.

Human Sight

Our eyes work just like a **camera**. When light enters our eyes, the rays are focussed on the retina, where an upside down image is formed. The brain then turns the image in the right way.

Colours are seen when certain wavelengths of light are reflected back and we see only those wavelengths. For example, the leaves of a tree absorb all the colours except the green colour. The green colour is reflected back into the atmosphere and when these rays enter our eyes we see that the *leaves are green*.

Uses of Light

1. Camera

A camera cannot work without light. It needs at least some amount of light to make an image.

2. Telescopes and Microscopes

Both telescopes and microscopes work with light. The position of the lenses inside them determine the size of the image formed.

3. Mirrors

Mirrors reflect light so that we can see an image. The image in a mirror is opposite of the original. The right hand appears left and the left hand appears right.

4. Periscope

A periscope bends light so that we can see an image. Periscopes use *lenses* and *mirrors* to form final image.

Periscope

5. Torches

Torches shine a beam of light so that we can see in the dark. Lighthouses also work as large torches that guide the ships at night.

There are two types of mirrors:

1. Convex Mirror

It is a mirror in which the reflective surface bulges towards the light source. Convex mirrors reflect the light outwards. The most common use of a convex mirror is the side view mirrors in cars. The mirrors show a larger area behind the car so that the driver can see behind the car. The objects in a convex mirror appear to be smaller than the actual object.

Reflection of light on convex mirror

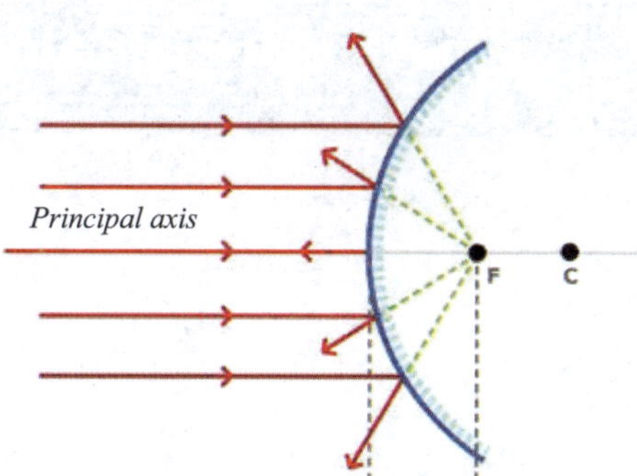

Convex Mirror

2. Concave Mirror

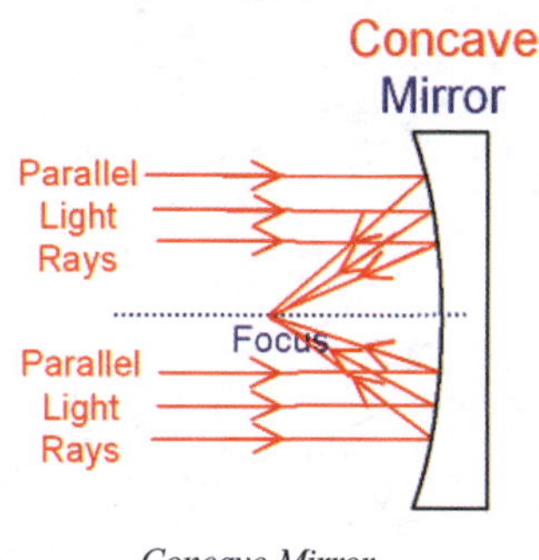

Concave Mirror

It is a mirror in which the reflective surface bulges inwards. Concave mirrors reflect the rays of light and focus them to a point which is called the **focal point**. Concave mirrors show a variety of image sizes depending upon the distance between the object and the mirror. A very common use of a concave mirror is a ***magnifying glass***. The object through a concave mirror looks larger than the actual object.

Quick Facts

- Fireflies emit their own light.
- Light is a form of energy that travels freely through space. This is called the electromagnetic radiation. Just like radio waves, infrared radiation and x-rays, we can only see a part of the range of elecromagnetic radiation, which is called the spectrum of light.
- A Rainbow is an arch formed by light refracted by drops of water diffused in the air.
- White materials reflect all light they receive and black materials absorb all light they receive.

Chapter - 7

SOUND

A sound is always caused by **vibration**. When an object vibrates, it causes the air particles to vibrate in the same rhythm. This way the vibration from the source of the sound reaches our ear and we can hear it. We can hear because the vibration in the air reach our ear drums and cause them vibrate too. This vibration is then analysed by our brain.

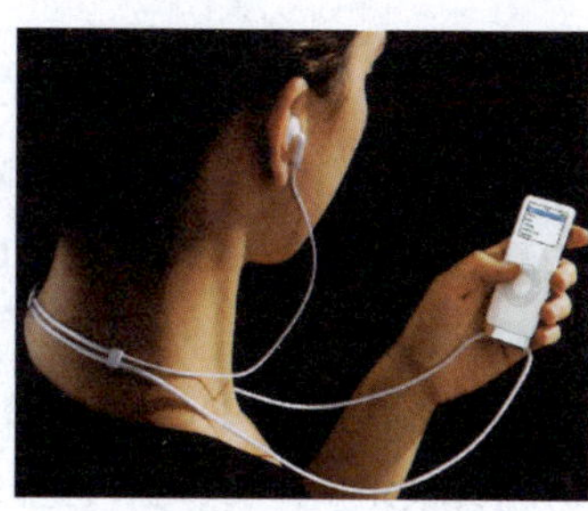

Sound Waves Entering the Ear

Sound can be transmitted through air, water and solids. Sound travels as a sound wave and it travels at different speeds in different mediums. Sound can also be *reflected, absorbed or refracted*.

Hard, glossy surfaces like glass, walls and ceramic tiles reflect sound and we hear an **echo**, whereas soft and porous surfaces like carpets and curtains absorb sound. Sound is refracted when the sound waves travel from one medium to another. For example, from air to liquid or from solid to liquid.

Sound always needs a medium to travel. In space, there is no sound because there is no air. Sound is measured in **decibels**. The hearing range is the range of frequencies that can be heard by a human or an

animal. Humans can usually hear voices in the range of 20hz to 20,000 hz. Although most animals can hear sounds up to a very high frequency, dogs can hear many sounds that humans cannot hear and bats emit sound in very high frequencies to help them navigate.

Speed of Sound

Though all sounds travel at the same speed, they travel faster in solids and liquids than through gases. **Supersonic jets** fly faster than the speed of sound. Therefore, they pass over you before you can hear the sound. An example to see that sound travels faster in solids is when you put your ear to a wall and knock on it. The vibration in your ear will be much more than the vibration when your ear is not near the wall.

Do it Yourself

Take a glass bottle with some liquid in it and another which is empty. Blow into the bottles and note the difference in the sound. When you blow into a bottle which has some liquid in it, you hear higher notes and when you blow into an empty bottle, you hear lower notes.

Echo

An echo is when sound is reflected from an object and then reaches our ears. Many animals use echo to locate their prey as well as navigate. Dolphins

Dolphins use Echo to Locate Preys

and whales produce sounds in the sea and when this sound reaches back to their ears reflected by some surface, they know whether they are heading towards another fish or a solid surface. Bats too use the same technique to navigate.

Types of Sound

1. **Ultrasound**

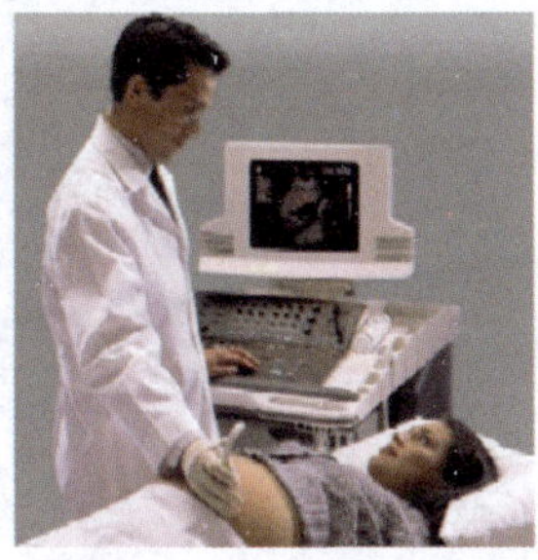

A Doctor doing Ultrasound

Ultrasound has a frequency higher than the upper limit of human hearing. The most common use of ultrasound is in **sonography** where pictures of a baby in the womb can be seen on a screen. Although prolonged exposure to ultrasound of very high frequency can be dangerous.

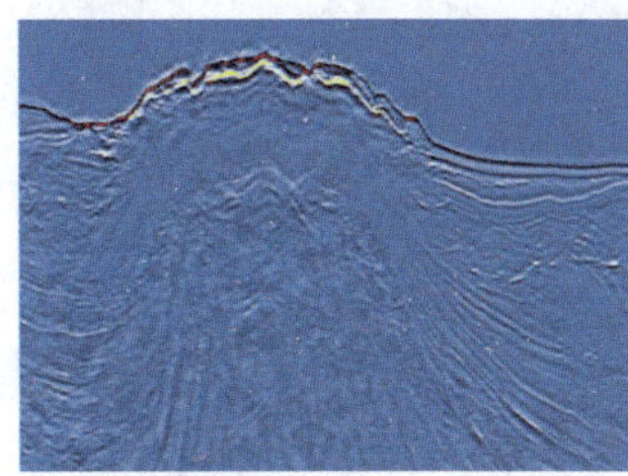

2. **Infrasound**

Infrasound is the sound that has a lower frequency than what the human ear can hear. Infrasound is commonly used for monitoring earthquakes, *charting rock and petroleum formations* below the surface of the Earth.

3. **Sound**

Humans Talk to Communicate

Sound is an important sense for living beings. It helps us to know our surroundings and to communicate. Sounds can soothe us, alarm us or warn us. Animals too use various types of sound to communicate with each other and sense danger.

Sonar

Sonar or **Sound Navigation** is a technique that uses sound to *navigate, communicate* or *detect underwater*. The frequency of Sonar can vary from Ultrasound to Infrasound. *Submarines* and *ships* use sonar to detect other vessels. Sonar is also used by Oceanologists to find out the depth of the sea at any given point.

Quick Facts

- **Sound comes from vibrations. These vibrations create sound waves which move through mediums, such as air and water before reaching our ears.**
- **Dogs can hear sound at a higher frequency than humans, allowing them to hear sounds that we cannot hear.**
- **Sound is used by many animals to detect danger, warning them of possible attacks before they happen.**
- **Sound can't travel through vacuum.**
- **The speed of sound is around 767 miles per hour (1,230 kilometres per hour). When travelling through water, sound moves around four times faster than when it travels through air.**
- **The scientific study of sound waves is known as Acoustics.**

Chapter - 8

HEAT

Every object contains atoms and molecules which are always moving about. The faster they move, the more energy the object has. We feel this energy as heat. When atoms are moving fast, the object is hot and when atoms are moving slow, the object is cold.

Heat always spreads from hotter things to cooler things. When you touch a hot object, the heat flows into your skin which triggers the sense cells and makes you feel hot. When you touch a cold object, heat from your skin flows to the object which triggers a cold feeling.

Heat is concerned with two things: temperature and the flow of heat. Temperature means the amount of thermal energy and flow of heat means the movement of thermal energy from place to place. The device that measures the temperature is called a **thermometer**.

Sources of Heat

1. Friction

Rubbing things together creates friction which in turn creates heat. When we rub our hands together, we feel that our hands have become warm.

Friction caused by Automobiles on Roads

2. Combustion

Burning Wood

Combustion or burning creates heat. When anything is burnt, it produces heat. Wood is burnt to produce heat in winters in many areas.

3. Electricity

Humans use electricity to create heat. Many appliances produce heat with electricity like ovens, geysers and heaters.

Room Heater

Geysers

An Electric Oven

Infrared Radiation

When heat escapes from warm objects, it travels in invisible rays like light. These rays are called infrared radiation. There are special cameras which capture these infrared radiation and create images. Hot areas appear white or red and cold areas appear black.

The natural source of heat for our planet is the sun. Heat from the sun travels to the Earth in the form of infrared radiation. Infrared rays are reflected away by white objects and absorbed by black objects. In desert areas, where the sunlight is very harsh, people paint their houses white to reflect the heat and keep their houses cool.

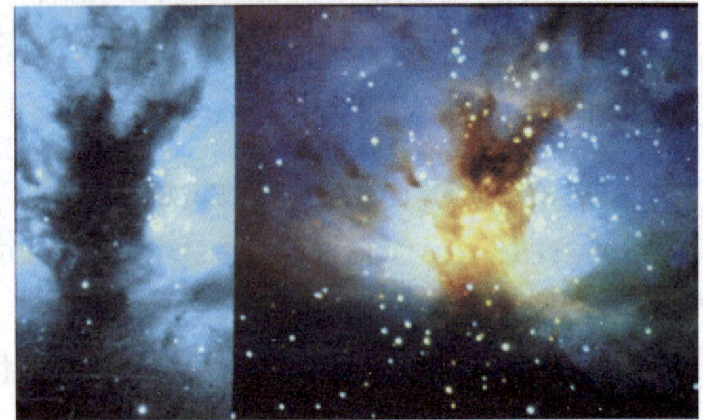
Infrared Radiation in the Atmosphere

Heat Transfer

Heat can be transferred from one object to another by *three processes*.

1. Conduction

Heat spreads from *hot objects to cooler objects*. When heat is transferred from one object to another through this process, its called *conduction*. The heat is transferred when two objects are in direct contact with each other. The better the conductor, the quicker will be the heat transfer. Example, When a metal object is brought in direct contact to a flame, the metal object becomes hot after some time.

Cooking Pan on Gas

2. Convection

A Hot Air Balloon

Convection is when heat is transferred by bulk motion of matter within fluids or gases. Convection cannot happen in solids as there cannot be bulk current flow. It is an up and down movement of liquids or gases. For example, A hot air balloon works when hot air within the balloon rises up because it is hotter than the colder air in the atmosphere.

3. Radiation

Electromagnetic waves travelling through space is called *radiation*. When these rays come in contact with an object, they transfer their heat to that object. Electromagnetic waves can travel through empty space. Example: A microwave uses electromagnetic waves to heat food.

A microwave uses electromagnetic waves to heat food

Points to Remember

When heat reaches an object, two things can happen; either the object experiences a rise in temperature or the substance changes its state. When you heat an iron rod, the temperature of the rod increases continuously. This happens because the molecules of iron start moving very fast.

In case you heat ice, it melts and becomes **water**. It changes its state. When ice melts into water, its temperature does not change. It is after the **ice** has changed into water that the temperature begins to rise and ultimately the water becomes **steam**.

Quick Facts

- Heat is the energy of moving molecules. The faster the molecules move, the hotter the substance is.
- Heat is the combined energy of all the moving molecules; temperature is how fast they are moving.
- The coldest temperature possible is absolute zero, or – 273°C, when molecules stop moving.
- When you heat a substance, its temperature rises because heat makes its molecules move faster.
- The specific heat of a substance is the energy needed in joules, to heat it by 1°C.
- Heat always spreads out from its source. It heats up its surroundings while cooling down itself.
- Heat moves in three different ways: conduction, convection and radiation.
- Good conducting materials such as, metals, silver, copper and gold feel cool to the touch because they carry heat away from your fingers quickly.

FORCE

In very simple words, *'force' is merely a push or a pull*. When you push or pull any object, you are using a force on it. Force can be exerted by touching and also otherwise like magnetism or gravity. *A force influences an object to undergo a change in speed, direction or shape.*

Gravitation

Gravitation is a natural phenomenon which is exerted by physical bodies with a force proportionate to their body mass. Gravitation is responsible for keeping the Earth and other planets in orbit around the Sun. The Moon also orbits the Earth because of this force. It is the most important force in the Universe.

Gravitation keeps the Earth, Sun and the Moon in Orbit

Magnetism

Magnet and Iron Nails

Magnetism is a force that is exerted by charged particles towards other particles. This force can make objects move by exerting force on them. Here it is not necessary for two objects to be in contact for the force to act. Example: When we bring a small magnet close to iron nails, the iron nails get attracted towards the magnet.

Centrifugal Force

When an object is travelling in a circular motion, it experiences an outward force. This force is called the **centrifugal force**. It depends on the mass of the object, the speed of rotation and the distance from the centre.

Example: On a merry-go-round, the riders feel a force that is pulling them outwards.

Do it Yourself

Downswing – Example of Centrifugal Force

Tie a string to a small pebble and start circling it on top of your head. Now if you release the string, the pebble will fall a little distance away from you instead of falling in a straight line downwards. It is because of the **centrifugal force**.

Friction

Friction acts in opposition to force. No matter in which direction an object is moving, friction pulls it the other way. Friction is the force which appears when two things are rubbing against each other. All objects are made up of atoms and molecules. No matter how smooth they look, if you look at them through a microscope, you will notice rough edges.

A Car on the Road

A Man Walking on the Road

When two objects are moving against each other, they are rubbing and grinding against each other, this is where friction comes from. But friction is very important for life to exist on the earth. It makes a lot of things simpler for us.

When we walk, friction prevents us from slipping. When we roll a ball on the floor, friction makes it stop after a while. Friction helps cars to steer on the road. Therefore, friction is not all that bad but useful for us. Friction slows down objects and in the process creates heat.

A Ball on the Ground

Thrust

Thrust is a force that acts in opposition to friction. The most common example is how a plane gains height. When an aeroplane takes off, there is a huge force of gravity that is pulling it down. To help the plane take off in the air, thrust plays an important role. When the fuel in the plane burns, it produces hot gases which expand and steam out from behind the aircraft. This force pushes the plane working against gravity and lifts the plane up in the air.

An Aeroplane Taking Off

Buoyancy

Rubber Duck Floating in a Tub

Buoyancy or floatation depends on how much water is pushing against an object in a certain situation. When any object is put into water, gravity pulls the object down and water in return exerts a force to keep that object up. If the object is lighter than water it will float, the force of buoyancy outweighs gravity and makes it float. In other words, if the total volume of the object is less than the total volume of water, then the object will float.

Example: When we put a rubber duck in a bathtub, it will float, but if we put a block of wood, it will drown. This is because the volume of the rubber duck is less than the volume of the water in the bathtub and the volume of the block of wood is more.

How do ships float?

A Ship Sailing in Sea

The shape of the ship is made into a hollow bowl or drum. By doing this, the total density of the ship is altered. So while the hollow part of the ship sinks, it displaces a large volume of water and therefore the ship floats on water. But if water starts entering the ship from any crack or opening, then the weight of the ship starts increasing causing the ship to sink.

Quick Facts

- Objects with mass are attracted to each other, this is known as gravity.
- Gravity keeps the Earth and other planets in our Solar System in orbit around the Sun. It also keeps the Moon in orbit around the Earth.
- Tides are caused by the rotation of the Earth and the gravitational effects of the Moon and the Sun.
- Because Mars has a lower gravity than the Earth, a person weighing 100kg on the Earth would only weigh 38kg on Mars.

Chapter - 10

MOTION

Everything in this universe keeps moving. It may be a very small movement in a very slow speed, but the movement is happening. Even when we are standing still, the earth is rotating around the sun and the sun is moving around our galaxy. There are several rules or laws that explain motion and the causes of change in motion.

Motion is all about forces. A force is always required to bring an object into motion. Force is also needed to make a body move faster and also to make it stop.

Newton's Laws of Motion

In 1687, **Sir Isaac Newton** worked out three important rules that explain how forces make things move. These laws work on everything and are the basics of all physical studies.

Newton's First Law of Motion

The Newton's First Law of Motion states *that an object at rest stays at rest and an object in motion stays in motion with the same speed and moves in the same direction unless an external force is acted upon it or applied to it*. There are two inertias:

inertia of rest and inertia of motion.

For example: A football will remain in the same position until you kick it.

Newton's Second Law of Motion

The Bigger the Force, the Greater will be Acceleration

The second law states that the acceleration of an object depends on two variables – the net force acting upon the object and the mass of the object.

The bigger the force and *the lighter the object, the greater will be the acceleration*. For example: A professional biker with a lightweight bike will accelerate faster than a normal person cycling a normal bike.

Newton's Third Law of Motion

Every Action has an Equal and Opposite Reaction

This law states that *every action has an equal and opposite reaction*. In other words, for every action, there is a reactional force that acts in the opposite direction. For example: if you press down on a stone with your finger, the stone also presses against your finger.

Speed and Velocity

Speed and velocity are two different things. Speed is how fast you are travelling, while velocity is how fast you travel in a particular direction. Changing direction without slowing reduces your velocity but the speed remains the same. Velocity is speed in a given direction. Speed is only how fast the object is moving, while velocity gives the speed and direction of an object. When a car is moving at a speed of 20km per hour on a circular path does not have the same velocity.

Inertia

Inertia is the resistance of any object to a change in its state of motion or rest. Inertia is proportional to the object's mass. In common words, *inertia is the amount of resistance to change in velocity*.

When any object is still or at rest, it will remain so until a force is applied to it. If you try and push a heavy object, it requires extra effort in the beginning, this is because of inertia. The object resists to change in its motion. In the same way, if an object is moving in a particular direction and you try to stop it, it takes effort to make it stop.

Experience Inertia

When you are sitting in a moving car and the car is moving at the speed of 50km/hr, you are also moving at 50km/hr. If the driver suddenly applies the breaks, you get a sudden jerk which is because of inertia. Your body is still moving at the same speed and resists the change in speed. That is why wearing seatbelts is necessary while driving or travelling in a car. The seatbelt pulls you back on the seat and prevents you from being thrown out of the car.

The Vehicle is in Inertia of Rest

Balanced and Unbalanced Forces

When two forces are acting upon an object with the same power, they balance each other. For example: When you are standing on the floor, there is a force exerted by gravity that pulls you down and a force exerted by the ground that pushes you upward. Thus, you remain standing on the ground. It is also called the *state of equilibrium* or *balanced force*.

Now take the same example, when you are standing on the floor in a state of equilibrium and someone comes and pushes you, you will fall on the other side. This is because other than the downward and the upward force, a third force from the side has been exerted and the equilibrium is disturbed. This is called an *unbalanced force*.

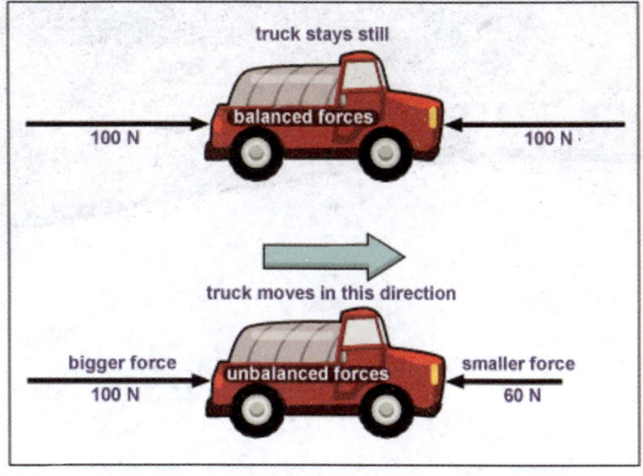

Balanced and Unbalanced Forces

Quick Facts

- **Distance is the actual length of the path covered by a body during whole journey, without taking into consideration its direction. It is a scalar quantity.**
- **Displacement is the distance in a particular direction. It is a vector quantity.**
- **Condition under which distance and displacement become same: When a body moves along a straight line in a positive direction, then its displacement and the distance travelled are equal and have the same sign.**
- **Speed is the rate of change of distance. Average speed is defined as the total distance travelled, divided by the total time taken.**
- **Scalar quantities are those which have magnitude only, but vector quantities have both magnitude and direction. For example, the amount of time and speed are scalar quantities because they have only magnitude, but acceleration and force are Vector quantities because they have magnitude and direction.**

Chapter - 11

MACHINES

A machine is an apparatus that *uses or applies mechanical power to perform a particular task*. Machines make tasks easier for us. They reduce the effort and time it takes to do a job. They work by either spreading the load or by concentrating your efforts.

Machines range from a few to a large number of parts according to the complication of the work to be done. *They are used instead of manual work to improve efficiency*.

There are six basic types of machines:

1. Lever

A lever is a simple machine. It may be a board or a bar that rests on a turning point. This turning point is called the **fulcrum**. The object that a lever moves is called the **load**. The closer the object is to the fulcrum, the easier it is to move it. Examples of lever are bottle openers, crowbars, etc.

Examples of Lever : A See-Saw

One type of lever works as a see-saw with the **fulcrum** between the **load** and the **effort**. When playing on a see-saw, you lift each other up and the lever makes it easier to do so.

Man Pushing a Load

Another type of lever places the load between the fulcrum and the effort. When you take things in a wheelbarrow, it makes it easier to move the load from one place to another.

A Type of Lever Tongs

A third type of a lever places the effort between the fulcrum and the load. When we use tongs, we press from the middle to make it more convenient to pick things.

2. Inclined Plane

An inclined plane is a flat surface that is higher on one end. It becomes easier to push or pull an object up a slope than lifting it straight up. An inclined plane makes the work of moving things easier. You need less energy and force to move objects with an inclined plane.

The Inclined Plane

The most common example of an inclined plane are slopes or ramps made instead of stairs. Using stairs requires more effort than using ramps. Therefore ramps are placed for climbing up or down for humans as well as cars, or for moving heavy loads.

3. Wheel and Axle

The axle is a rod that goes through the centre of the wheel. Together, they work as a rotating machine that makes it easier to move things from one place to the other.

A Cart Drawn by a Man

Wheels and axle are what make automobiles move. We all know that wheels make moving easier, so everything from a bicycle to an aeroplane has wheels and axle. Small carts that are used for moving goods everyday are simple examples of wheel and axle. Using this machine minimises the effort and force for moving loads. Roller skates, door knobs, watches, clocks, all use this simple machine to work.

4. Screw

Cockscrew Jar Lid

A screw is a machine made out of another machine. It is actually an inclined plane that winds around itself. A screw has ridges, it is not smooth like a nail. Screws are used to lower or raise things and also to hold objects together.

Clamp

Screws are used in jacks, key rings, clamps, light bulbs and jar lids. Also a corkscrew is a simple machine that helps in opening the lid of a bottle. It is easier to twist a corkscrew into the cork and then pull it open than putting a spike in and pulling it.

5. Wedge

Knife

Axe

Nails

A wedge is used to push two objects apart. It is made up of two inclined planes. These planes meet and form a sharp edge. This edge can split things apart. *An axe, a knife, a nail and a fork are all wedges.* All of them have a sharp edge and are used to push things apart.

6. Pulley

A Well with a Pulley

A pulley is a machine that is used to pull something. It is made up of a wheel and a rope. One part of the rope is attached to the load. When you pull on one side of the pulley, the wheels turn and move the load. A pulley helps to move things up, down or sideways. These are best used for areas that are hard to reach and make the task of moving heavy objects easier.

A Crane

A crane is the most common example of a pulley. Cranes are used to move very heavy objects in industries. A simple pulley is used to get water out of a well.

Quick Facts

- **The Lever has three parts:**
  - **Resistance force, or load – what is being moved or lifted**
  - **Effort force – the force that the lever exerts, or the work done on the lever**
  - **Fulcrum – the fixed pivot point**
- **The Wheel and Axle**
  - **When either the wheel or the axle turns, the other part also turns.**
  - **One complete turn of the wheel produces one complete turn of the axle.**
  - **If the wheel turns but the axle doesn't, it is not a wheel-and-axle machine.**

Chapter - 12

GRAVITY

Gravity is the pull towards the centre of the earth. In other words, it is a force that any two objects in this universe have towards each other. On the earth, it is the force that pulls us towards the earth. It is because of gravity that we can stand on the earth. When we jump, the force of gravity reduces our speed and then pulls us down back on the ground after reaching the highest point that we can.

Gravitational Force : An Apple Falling on the Ground

Sir Isaac Newton first mentioned gravity. His law of gravity defines the attractive force between all objects that have **mass**. The famous story of an apple falling on Newton's head is not true, but he did see an apple falling from a tree on the ground and wondered why.

Isaac Newton's Law of Universal Gravitation

This law states that bodies with mass attract each other with a force that varies directly as a product of their masses and inversely as the square of distance between them.

The Newton's Law of Universal Gravitation is mathematically expressed as $F = G (m_1m_2/ r^2)$.

The Earth as a Giant Magnet

Although the origin of the Earth's magnetic field is not known, but scientists have formulated theories which tell us about the magnetic field of the earth.

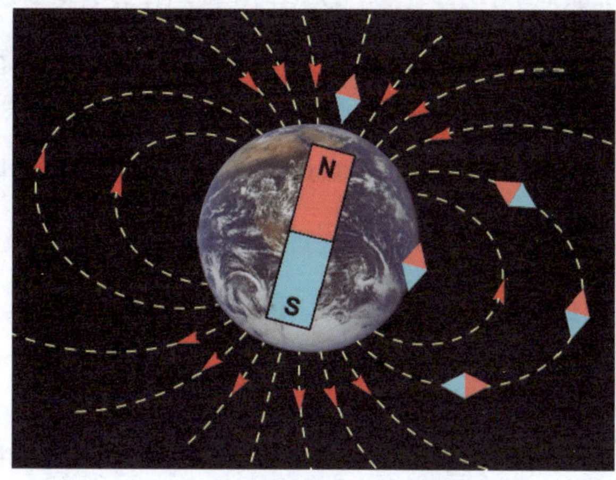

The Earth's Magnetic Field

The planet, Earth is a giant magnet tilted on its axis. You can imagine it as if the earth has a giant bar of magnet in its centre. The slight tilt is called **declination**. On the surface though the magnetic field is very weak; this is obvious because of the size of our planet.

The earth's core consists of molten iron but at the centre, the pressure is so great that the iron becomes a solid. **Radiation** from this heat and the **rotation** of the earth cause the molten iron to move in a rotational pattern.

These rotational forces tend to weaken the earth's magnetic field around the axis of the spin. A magnetic field is created by the motion of electrical charges and thus in the same way, the magnetic field of the earth is created.

Sea Birds

Gravity plays a very important role in making the earth as it is. **Tides**, which are important factors of the oceans, are caused by the *rotation of the earth* and *the gravitational forces of the sun and the moon*.

Gravity affects all living beings. Life began from the sea. Some aquatic animals still use gravity as their directional cue. Land species adapted to the gravitational forces and evolved. Birds too get influenced by the force of gravity when they fly. They have wings larger than their bodies so that they can lift off the ground.

So gravity is not just a phenomenon that happens on the earth, but it also affects us a lot. All the planets of the solar system as well as our sun have gravitational forces that together make the world that we see.

Build Your Own Magnet

Things You Will Need

1. A needle or a wire like a piece of steel.
2. Something small that floats like a piece of cork, a piece of plastic or a piece of Styrofoam coffee cup.
3. A dish 9-12 inches in diameter with about an inch of water in it.

Step 1: The first step is to turn the needle into a magnet. This can be done with the help of another magnet. Strike the magnet along the needle 10 to 20 times.

Making A Magnet

Step 2: Next place the needle on the piece of cork, plastic or the Styrofoam coffee cup.

Step 3: Then place the piece of cork, plastic or the Styrofoam in the water in the dish.

Your compass will slowly point towards the north.

How Does This Work?

Making a lightweight object float on water creates a nearly frictionless bearing and therefore, your magnet works.

Quick Facts

- Gravity is a force. It is the force that keeps our feet on the ground and the Earth spinning around the Sun.
- All objects have gravity. The bigger the object, the stronger the gravity.
- Because Mars has a lower gravity than the Earth, a person weighing 100kg (220 pounds) on Earth would only weigh 38kg (84 pounds) on Mars. The surface gravity n mars is about 38% of the surface gravity on Earth.
- Objects with mass are attracted to each other, and this is known as gravity.

Chapter - 13

ATOMIC AND NUCLEAR ENERGY

Atomic Physics is the area of Physics which studies the arrangement of electrons around a nucleus and the processes by which these arrangements change. It deals with the atom as a system of nucleus and electrons.

Nuclear Physics is the area of Physics that is concerned with the atomic nuclei alone.

The Atom

An atom consists of *protons with positive charge*, equal and opposite to that of *electrons with negative charge*, and *neutrons with charge zero*; together these are called the **nucleons**.

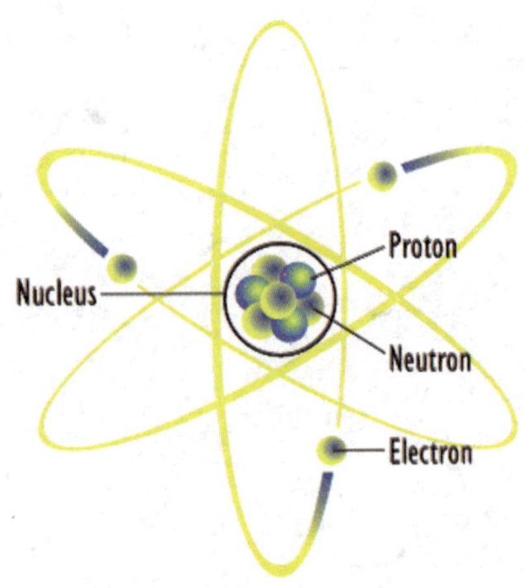

The Constituents of an Atom

Protons and neutrons are responsible for most of the atomic mass. Both protons and neutrons reside in the nucleus. Electrons reside in orbits around the nucleus.

Atomic Energy/Nuclear Energy

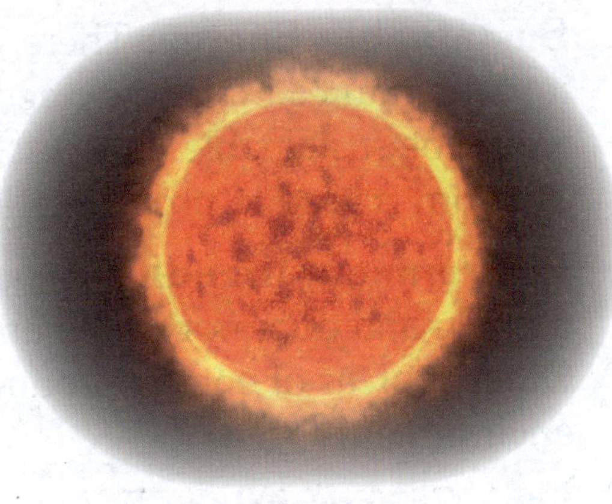

The Sun (Atomic Energy)

Atomic energy is the energy produced by atoms. Atoms have immense amount of energy stored in them. Nuclear reactions are caused by harnessing atomic energy.

The sun is the most common example of atomic energy. In the sun, **fusion reaction** takes place in which hydrogen is continuously fusing and making **helium**. As a result of this **nuclear reaction**, atomic energy is produced.

Atomic Bomb or Atom Bomb

The Atomic Bombing at Hiroshima and Nagasaki (Japan)

Hydrogen atom when bombarded with neutron split into two and produce atomic energy. This is what happens in an **atomic bomb**. A **hydrogen bomb** or atomic bombs are the most destructive weapons.

Nuclear Energy

In nuclear plants, **uranium** is broken down by neutron hitting on its nuclei and a continuous process of splitting uranium begins which is called **chain reaction**. This process of producing nuclear energy causes a long-term *fuel fulfilment*.

Advantages of Nuclear Energy

Sustainable Energy: There is a threat that oil reserves will finish in near future. Scientists needed to find a source of energy that would be sustainable. In a nuclear reaction, a very small amount of uranium is used to produce a lot of energy.

Environment-friendly: A nuclear power plant is environment-friendly and does not create any type of pollution outside the plant. Other sources of energy produce a lot of pollution and damage the environment.

Less Consumption: For producing nuclear energy, a very small amount of uranium is needed, while in other processes, a large amount of oil or coal are needed to produce the same amount of energy. Therefore, nuclear energy is also a cheap source of energy.

No by-products: When producing nuclear energy, no by-products like CO_2 or CO are formed, whereas, while producing energy from coal or oil, large amounts of waste products are produced. In case of nuclear energy, the only by-product is **water**.

Disadvantages of Nuclear Energy

Explosive: Nuclear reactions are dangerous. Without proper preventive measures, producing nuclear energy can be destructive.

Nuclear Waste: Radiation continues to come out of the waste also. This radiation is so harmful that it can kill only by touching. Therefore, it is very important to keep the waste restricted within the power plant.

Nuclear Energy Ends: A nuclear plant cannot keep giving energy forever. Around half a decade is the life of a nuclear power plant.

Radiation: There is a large amount of radiation produced in nuclear reactions. This radiation in the long run is harmful for living beings. The term used for radiation emitting from an atom is **meltdown**.

Quick Facts

- In World War II, two atomic bombs or atom bombs were dropped in Hiroshima and Nagasaki in Japan. These are the only incidents of using atomic bombs up to date. An atomic bomb was dropped on Hiroshima on 6th August, 1945 and on Nagasaki on 9th August, 1945. These bombings killed about 90,000 to 1,66,000 people in Hiroshima and around 60,000 to 80,000 people in Nagasaki.
- Nuclear energy is energy that is released either by splitting atomic nuclei or by forcing the nuclei of atoms together.
- Nuclear energy comes from mass-to-energy conversions that occur in the splitting of atoms. Albert Einstein's famous mathematical formula, $E = mc^2$ explains this. The equation says: E [energy] equals to m [mass] times c^2, in which [c stands for the speed or velocity of light]. This means that nuclear is mass multiplied by the square of the velocity of light.
- Nuclear energy is produced by a controlled nuclear chain reaction and creates heat, energy which is used to boil water, produce steam, and drive a steam turbine.
- Nuclear power can come from the fission of uranium, plutonium or thorium or the fusion of hydrogen into helium. Today it is almost all uranium.
- Nuclear power plants need less fuel than ones which burn fossil fuels. One ton of uranium produces more energy than that is produced by several million tons of coal or several million barrels of oil.
- In France, nuclear power is the most widespread, supplying around 80 percent of the country's electricity.

Chapter - 14

PRESSURE

Pressure is defined as *force per unit area*. The standard unit for pressure is **Pascal**. If an object is on a surface, the force pressing on the surface is the weight of the object, but if kept differently, it might have a different area contact with the surface and therefore, exert a different pressure.

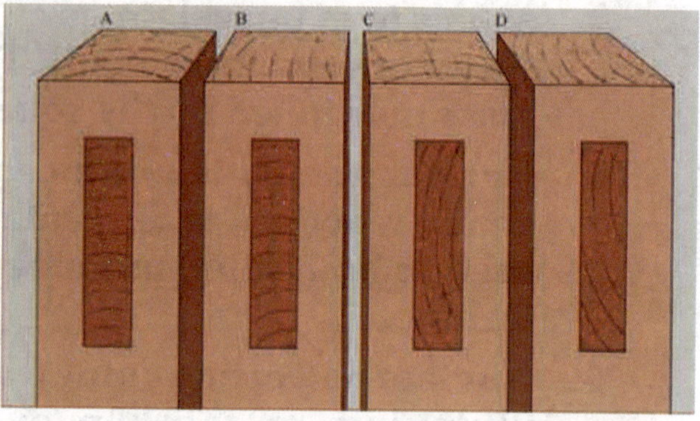

The Force Pressing on the Surface Area is the Weight

When peeling an apple, the edge of the knife is kept the sharpest so that the force applied to peel the apple may reduce. Less force will be required if the knife is sharp. Similarly, when putting an injection, the sharper the point of the needle, the lesser the force required to inject it.

In both the above examples, the surface area is reduced and therefore, the force applied becomes lesser.

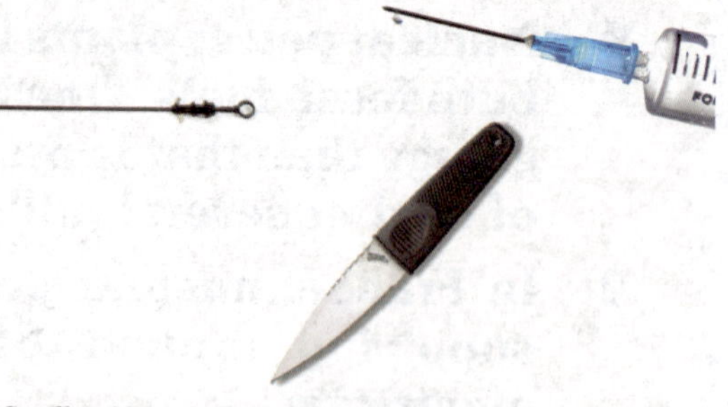

Smaller Objects like Needle, Knife are Lighter in Weight

Types of Pressure

1. Fluid Pressure

It is the pressure at some point within a fluid. This can occur in two situations: An open condition, like the ocean, swimming pool, etc or a closed condition, like water line or gas line.

Pressure in an open condition is said to be **static** because the motion creates very little changes in pressure. Pressure in closed conditions is static when the fluid is not moving and **dynamic** when the fluid can move.

2. Explosion Pressure

It is the pressure as a result of igniting gases in confined and open spaces.

3. Negative Pressure

When a closed area has lower pressure than the area around it, it is called negative pressure. Pipelines normally have a negative pressure. This is done so because when oil or petrol pipelines go below the water in oceans, the negative pressure helps the oil not to get spilled in water. Therefore, negative pressure prevents oil spills that can be dangerous.

4. Stagnation Pressure

It is the maximum pressure experienced by a fluid. A fluid exerts stagnation pressure when it is forced to stop moving.

5. Surface Pressure

It is the atmospheric pressure at a location on the earth's surface. It is directly proportional to the mass of the air over that location.

6. Vapour Pressure

It is the pressure resulting from evaporation of a liquid in a closed container. As the temperature increases, the vapour pressure also increases, and conversely as the temperature decreases, vapour pressure also decreases.

7. Liquid Pressure

Liquids exert pressure due to the distribution of their own weight. The pressure depends upon the depth of the fluid, the density of the fluid and the acceleration of gravity.

Do it Yourself

To see the impact of liquid pressure, do this experiment.

Plastic Bottle with 3 Holes

Take a big plastic soft drink bottle and make three holes on its side vertically and equally distant from each other.

Close the holes with your fingers and fill the bottle with water up to the top. Release the holes and observe how the water falls out of the holes.

You will observe that the water from the bottom hole comes out with the fastest speed and goes the farthest. While from the middle hole, it goes a little less and from the top hole, the least further.

Water from Bottom Hole Comes Out the Fastest

This happens because of the pressure that water is exerting. At the bottom the pressure is the highest and therefore, the water comes out with the most pressure and goes the farthest.

An Astronaut with Hammer

Quick Facts

- The deeper you go in an ocean, the higher is the pressure. That is why deep sea divers have to wear special suits to protect themselves from the high pressure.
- Air pressure varies constantly from place to place and from time to time as the sun's heat varies.
- Air pressure is measured with a device called a barometer in millibars.
- Normal air pressure at sea level is 1013 mb, but it can vary from between 800 mb and 1050 mb.
- Barometers are used to detect changes in air pressure. The first barometer was invented by Evangelista Toricelli in 1644.
- Air pressure is shown on weather maps with lines called isobars, which join together places of equal pressure.
- High-pressure zones are called anticyclones, whereas the low-pressure zones are called cyclones, or depressions.
- A fall in air pressure warns that stormy weather is on its way, because depressions are linked to storms.

Chapter - 15

MIRRORS AND REFLECTION

Mirror

A mirror is simply an object that reflects light. To understand a mirror, first we have to understand light. We know that light travels in a straight line until an obstruction comes in between. When light hits a surface, it is either absorbed or reflected back. Mirrors are objects that reflect light.

Mirror

The common mirror found in our houses is a sheet of glass attached to a thin layer of metallic backing. This mirror shows our reflection left-right. Actually, what mirrors show is the front and back. When you write something on paper and see it against the light, you see front and back. But mirrors are used for a lot more purposes than to admire ourselves.

Mirrors are used as per how they reflect light. **According to their make, there are two basic types of mirrors:**

1. Concave Mirrors

Concave mirrors curve inwards. When light is reflected, it is focussed at one point which is called the **focal point**. From far, the image will look upside down, but as you come closer to the mirror, the image will become straight.

Concave mirrors make an image that is larger than the actual object. Concave mirrors are used in a variety of things. Concave mirrors are used in *shaving mirrors, automobile headlights, telescopes*.

Reflection of Light on Concave Mirror

2. Convex Mirror

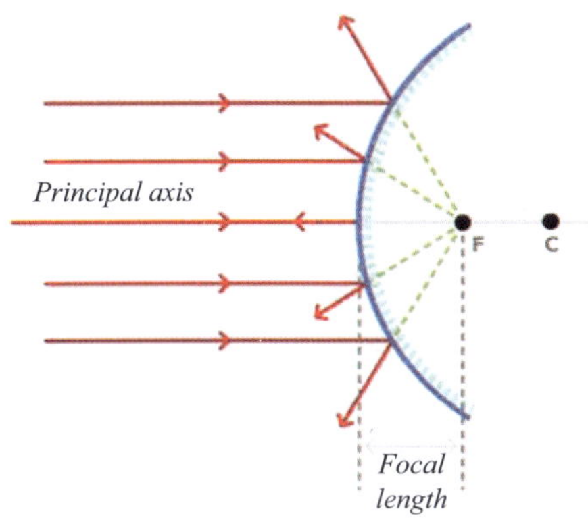

Reflection of Light on Convex Mirror

A convex mirror bulges outwards. It reflects light at a wide angle and creates an image that is slightly distorted and smaller in size than the actual object. They also cover a large area.

Convex mirrors are smaller in size and show a larger area and that is why they are used in safety mirrors. The rear view mirrors in cars is a convex mirror that shows the driver the area behind the car. It is often seen on rear view mirrors that objects are closer than they appear. Convex mirrors are also used in streetlights so as to converge light to a larger area and in *surveillance cameras*.

Surveillance Cameras

There are also other types of mirrors that are used specifically for certain things. Other types of mirrors are:

1. Non-reversing Mirror

A Non-reversing Mirror

A non-reversing mirror creates an image like a normal mirror except that it is not reversed. Left is left and right is right in the image formed by the non-reversing mirror.

A non-reversing mirror is made by joining two normal mirrors at their edges at an angle of 90 degrees. If the joint is positioned vertically and you look into the angle, you will see a non-reversed image. The problem though is that there is a line that interrupts your viewing that is made by joining two mirrors.

2. Acoustic Mirror

An Acoustic Mirror

An acoustic mirror is used to reflect sound instead of light. It is a huge concrete disk which reflects and distributes sound. It is in the shape of a concave mirror, curving inwards. The US Army used acoustic mirrors before the invention of radars as a *warning system against air attacks*.

3. Two-way Mirrors

Two-way Mirrors

A two-way mirror is made by coating one side of the sheet of glass with a very thin material that lightly reflects light. When the coated side faces the lighted room, some light is reflected back and some goes into the darker room behind the mirror. Therefore, you can see into the lighted room, but not out of it. Almost no light goes from the dark side to the light side and also almost no light is reflected from the dark side. Most of the light comes in from the light side. People on *the dark side see a window and people on the light side see a mirror.*

Two- sided mirrors are most commonly used in interrogation rooms, where policemen can watch the interrogation from another room and the persons being interrogated cannot see outside.

Quick Facts

- **When you look in a mirror, you can see yourself because the light bounces straight back to you. Light travels in straight lines. When a beam of light hits a mirror, it bounces off like a snooker ball does when it hits the edge of the table. Light that hits the mirror straight on, bounces straight back along the same path.**
- **The history of mirror can be traced back to the ancient times, when people first noticed their reflection in water bodies, such as ponds and rivers. At that time, they used to consider it magic. Ancient Greeks, Egyptian and Romans are believed to have used the mirror for the first time. It comprised of a disk of metal, with a face that was highly polished to reflect an image. Usually, the mirror carried a handle and at times, some designing on the back.**
- **The first used mirrors were made of molten bronze or copper and were round, oval or square in shape. These mirrors were polished to new, whenever rust developed. Later, mirrors were also made of tin, silver and even gold, in ancient Rome.**

Chapter - 16

RELATIVITY

Sir Albert Einstein

Relativity includes two theories of Albert Einstein; General Relativity and Special Relativity. The Theory of Relativity changed the concept of motion by saying all motions are relative.

Special Relativity

Special relativity is the theory of the structure of space-time. Special relativity is based on two things: All uniform motion is relative and there is no well-defined state of rest and the speed of light is the same for all initial observers regardless of the state of motion of the source.

Special relativity shows that the measurements of distance and time depend on how fast you are travelling. It also shows that as an object travels faster, its mass increases. And as the mass increases, it takes more and more energy to increase its speed. When the object reaches the speed of light, its mass becomes so great that no more energy can increase its speed. This concludes that the speed of light is the universal speed limit which nothing with mass can break.

Time Dilation

An example of time dilation is that if a person A moves faster than a person B, person A will experience time at a slower rate, and the clock he is carrying will tick slower than the watch of person B.

Twin Paradox

Twin paradox shows how time changes because of speed and mass. The faster something moves, the more mass they have, and the slower time passes for them.

General Relativity

General relativity is the theory of the behaviour of space and time. *It is the theory of gravitation by Einstein. It was published in its final form in 1916.* Einstein proposed that the space time is curved. His equations relate the curvature of space-time with the mass, energy and momentum within it.

Milky Way Galaxy

Newton's theory described gravity as a force. The Earth exerts this force on all matter on the earth. In general relativity, it is said that space and time are dynamic that can curve in response to the effects of matter.

Before this theory of relativity was made, most physicists believed that the universe was unchanging or static. After Einstein developed his theory, physicists thought to apply it to the universe. They applied the equations of space and time to the universe and these predicted that the universe was either *expanding or contracting*.

General relativity adds gravity to special relativity. It has been shown that time passes slowly near heavy objects.

In 1929, **Edwin Hubble** observed that all distant galaxies appeared to be moving away from us just like the way predicted by the general relativity.

Sir Edwin Hubble

Quick Facts

- Matter determines how space curves. Curved space determines how matter moves.
- Einstein's General Theory of Relativity explains gravitation as distortion of the structure of space-time by matter, affecting the inertial motion of other matter. (Inertia is the resistance of a physical object to a change in its state of motion, represented numerically by its mass.)
- Due to natural curvature of space, the shortest path between any two objects is never a straight line, but a curved line called a geodesic. An example of this is that we can see stars that are located in a straight line behind the sun appearing near the edge of the sun. This occurs because the strong gravitational effect of the sun curves space in such a way that the shortest distance for light to travel is the geodesic path curves around the edge of the sun. An earth-based analogy is that aeroplane flight paths follow geodesic paths instead of straight lines around the curved earth's surface to save both time and fuel.

Exercises

I. Answer the following questions.

1. What is energy and what are the different types of energy?
2. What is energy conversion? Explain with the context of coal.
3. What is an electric charge? Explain any three different ways of producing Electricity.
4. What is an electric current? What are the types of electric currents?
5. What do you understand by electrification by friction?
6. List a few uses of electricity.
7. What are magnets and what is a magnetic field?
8. What are electromagnets?
9. What is a spectrum? What are the seven different waves in our light spectrum?
10. What are Ultraviolet Rays, X-Rays and Gamma Rays?

II. Fill in the blanks with suitable word(s).

1. A sound is always caused by __________.
2. An __________ has a frequency higher than the upper limit of human hearing.
3. An ____________ is the sound that has a lower frequency than what the human ear can hear.

4. Sonar is a technique that uses sound to _________.
5. _____________ or burning creates heat.
6. Heat spreads from hotter objects to cooler objects. This process is called ______________
7. ____________ is when heat is transferred by bulk motion of matter within fluids or gases.
8. Electromagnetic waves travelling through space are called _________.

III. Match the two columns correctly.

A	B
1. Gravitation is responsible for keeping the	atomic energy.
2. An atom consists of protons, electrons and neutrons	to a change in its state of motion or rest.
3. The sun is the most common example of	in opposition to force.
4. Inertia is the resistance of any object	the earth and other planets in orbit around the sun.
5. Friction acts	and together, they are called nucleons.

IV. Multiple Choice Questions (MCQs)

1. The standard unit for pressure is _____________.

   a. Newton b. Pascal c. Joule

2. Thrust is a force that acts in opposition to _____________.

   a. Friction b. Gravitation c. Inertia

3. Concave mirrors make an image that is _____________.

   a. larger than the actual object

b. smaller than the actual object

c. of the same size

4. A convex mirror bulges ______________.

a. outwards b. inwards

c. both outwards and inwards

5. An acoustic mirror is used to reflect ______________.

a. light b. sound instead of light

c. sound and light

6. The Theory of Relativity was propounded by ____________.

a. Thomas Edison b. Albert Einstein

c. Edwin Hubble

7. Air pressure is measured with a device called __________.

a. Barometer b. Thermometer

c. Anemometer

8. A fall in air pressure warns that a ______________.

a. stormy weather is on its way

b. sunny weather is on its way

c. cloudy weather is on its way

9. The deeper you go in an ocean, the higher the ____________.

a. temperature b. volume c. pressure

10. A Hydrogen atom when bombarded with neutron splits into two and produces ______________.

a. atomic energy b. nuclear energy

c. electrical energy

Glossary

Environment: Surroudnings, atmosphere

Quantitative: That is or may be estimated by quantity

Analysis: A system of calculation, the process or method of studying the nature of something

Survive: Exist, to remain alive

Transform: To change in form, appearance, or structure

Transfer: To convey or remove from one place, person, etc. to another

Conservation: The careful utilisation of a natural resource in order to prevent depletion

Exert: To apply force, to put forth or into use

Manipulate: To manage or influence skilfully

Retrieve: To recover or regain

Emit: To give forth, or to send forth, discharged

Penetrate: To enter and diffuse itself through, permeate

Exposure: An act of revealing or unmasking

Wavelenght: The distance measured in the direction of propagation of a wave

Medium: An intervening substance, as air

Merely: Simply, entirely, purely

Magnify: Enlarge

Variables: Changeable

Vibrate: Shake vigorously

Navigate: To move through water

CHEMISTRY

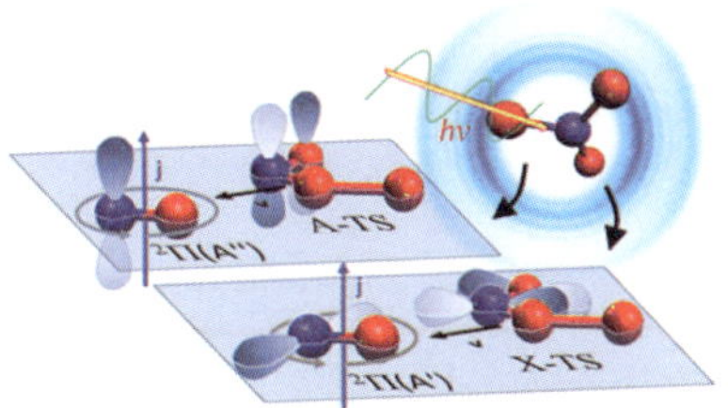

Chapter - 1

MATTER

Everything around us is made up of matter. *A 'matter' is any type of material and anything that has mass, and takes up space*. Matter is also related to light and *electromagnetic radiation*. It includes things we can see as well as we cannot see, such as tables, chairs, boxes, men, women, plants, animals, etc., and are matter or objects that we can see, but gases like Hydrogen (H_2), Oxygen (O_2), Nitrogen(N_2), etc., are matter that we cannot see, yet they occupy space and volume. *Hence, Matter is anything made up of atoms and molecules that has mass or weight and occupies space or volume.*

An Astronaut in Space

A Table and Chairs

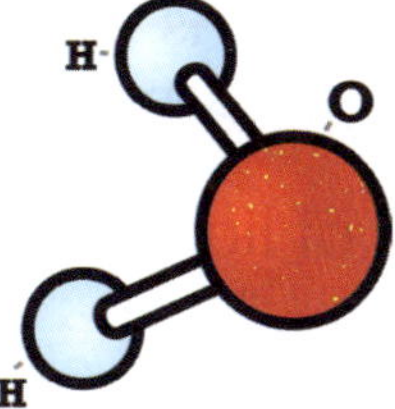

Two Hydrogen Atoms and A Molecule of Oxygen combine to form H_2O or Water Molecule

Two atoms of Hydrogen and one atom of Oxygen combine to form a molecule of Water or H_2O.

Types of Matter

There are **four** main types of matter. All of these behave differently because the particles in their makeup move in different ways.

1. Solid

Atoms/Molecules in a Solid

A solid has a definite shape and volume. A solid object is rigid. The atoms and molecules in a solid are tightly packed together and are not compressible.

Stone (A Solid)

Examples of solids are: All the things like rock, wood, television, computer, that are hard to touch and cannot be compressed etc.

2. Liquid

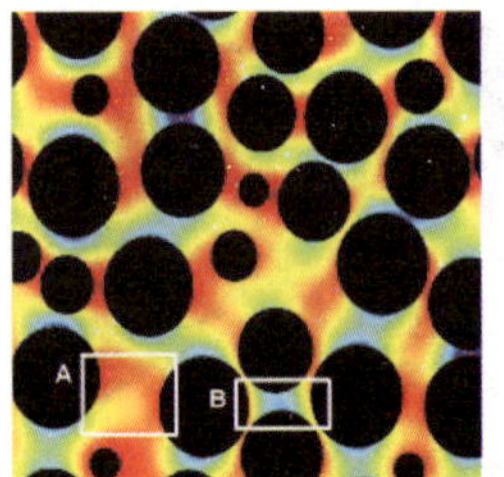

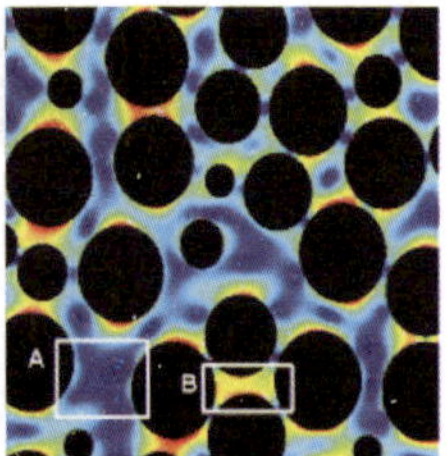

Atoms/Molecules in a Liquid

A liquid does not have a definite shape, but they do have a definite volume. A liquid takes the shape of its container. Its molecules are further apart than that of solids. They change their shape by flowing. Since the atoms and molecules touch each other, the density of a liquid is close to that of a solid.

Water (A Liquid)

Examples of liquids are: All the things like water, oil, honey, that take the shape of their container etc.

3. Gases

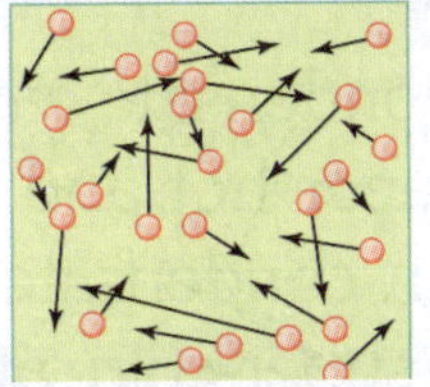

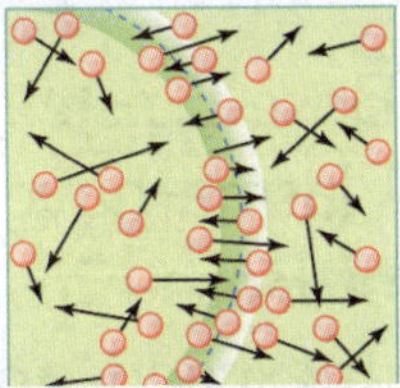

Atoms/Molecules in a Gas

Gases have neither a definite shape nor a definite volume. If confined, gases take the shape of their container and if left out, they spread out in the atmosphere. The atoms and molecules of gases are spread out resulting in a very low density and have enough energy to overcome attractive forces.

A Balloon filled with Air

Examples of gases are: Oxygen, Hydrogen, Helium, Nitrogen, Air, etc. We cannot see gases until we see their container or they have a particular colour. A way to see a gas is by blowing up a balloon. The air we blow into it takes the shape of the balloon and it blows up.

4. Plasma

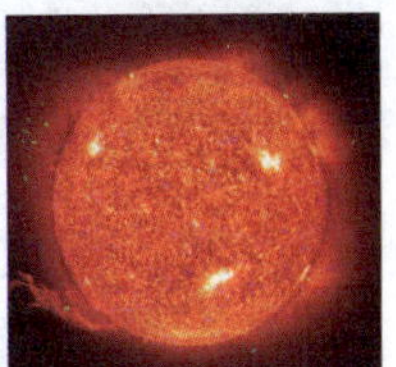

Plasma

Plasma has neither a definite shape nor a definite volume. Plasma can be achieved by heating and ionizing a gas. Free electrical charges make plasma electrically conductive. Plasma has some properties of liquids and some of gases. It is the most common state of matter in our universe and most of it is not visible.

Lightning

Examples of plasma are: It exists inside the sun, stars are made up of plasma, lightning is also a type of plasma. You can also find plasma inside *fluorescent lights*, *lightning* and *neon signs*.

Bose-Einstein Condensate

Two scientists, Satyendra Bose and Albert Einstein had predicted this fifth state of matter in 1920. At that time, they did not have the equipment and facilities to create it. In 1995, two scientists, Cornell and Wieman finally created this new state of matter called BEC (Bose–Einstein Condensate).

Bose-Einstein condensate can be said to be the opposite of plasma. Plasma have super hot and super excited atoms, while the atoms of Bose-Einstein condensate are totally opposites, they are super-unexcited and super-cold atoms. At a certain temperature, near zero atoms clump together and they no longer remain many atoms, but take on the same qualities and become one *blob*. Cornell and Weiman did this with an element called *Rubidium*.

Quick Facts

- **A place where there is no matter at all is called a vacuum. The best example of a vacuum is the space between stars.**
- **Particles in a gas vibrate and move freely at high speed. Particles in a liquid vibrate, move about, and slide past each other, and particles in a solid vibrate (jiggle) but generally do not move from place to place.**
- **Changes, such as pressure and temperature, can alter the states of matter, whether solids, liquids or gases.**
- **Most everyday matter, occurs as mixtures which are combination of two or more substances. For example: In water, two atoms of Hydrogen combine with one atom of Oxygen to form the chemical formula: H_2O.**
- **When solid matter changes to a liquid, it is called melting and when liquid changes to a gas, it is called sublimation.**
- **When liquids change to a gas, it is also called vaporization and when liquids change to solids, it is called freezing. When a gas changes to plasma, it is called ionization.**

Chapter - 2

PROPERTIES OF MATTER

There are so many types of materials around us, all have different properties. Some materials are *colourful*, some are *brittle*, some are *very hard* and some may be *transparent*. All these different features are called *properties*.

There are many different properties on which materials can be classified:

1. Boiling Point

Boiling point is the hottest state a liquid can get before it changes into a gas. When a liquid is heated, it reaches a temperature, where vapour from inside the liquid rises. Once the liquid starts to boil, the temperature remains constant until all of the liquid has been converted into gas.

Boiling Water in a Pan

2. Freezing Point

The freezing point is the temperature at which a liquid becomes a solid. When a liquid is cooled, it reaches a temperature, where its atoms and molecules become tightly packed like that of a solid.

Although liquids can be frozen beyond their freezing points, and then they are called *supercooled*.

Ice Cubes in an Ice Tray

Lighted Candles with Wax Melting

3. Melting Point

The melting point is the temperature at which a solid turns into a liquid. When a solid is heated, it reaches a temperature, where its atoms and molecules start to move around and it turns into a liquid.

4. Conductivity

A Utensil on a Gas

Conductivity is how well a material can let electricity or heat travel through it.

Heat is transferred from a hot body to a cold one and electricity is transferred by a charged body to a neutral one.

Materials that are good at conduction are called **conductors**. Materials that do not conduct heat or electricity are called **insulators**. Aluminium or steel are good conductors of heat and are therefore used in cooking utensils. Copper or aluminium are good conductors of electricity and therefore are used to make electrical wires.

Copper Wire (Conductor)

5. Flammability

Flammability is how easily or quickly a material catches fire. We use materials as per their flammability. For cooking, we always use materials that are not flammable like aluminium which is a

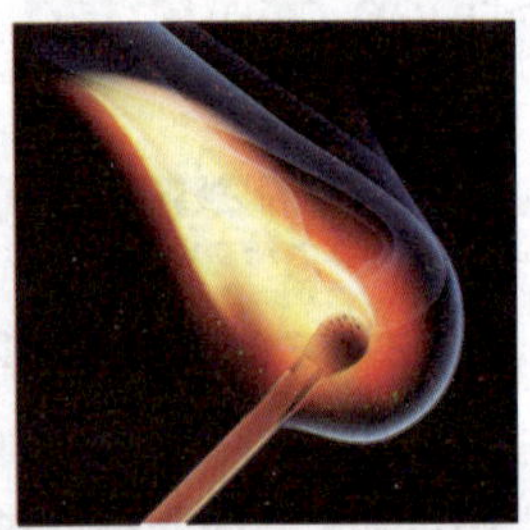

A Matchstick Burning

good conductor of heat but does not burn. If we use a cloth to cook food, then it will catch fire. In the opposite case, if we want to light a fire, we use a material that burns like wood.

6. Flexibility

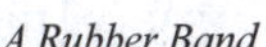

A Rubber Band

An Eraser

Flexibility is how easily a material can be bent. It is the rigidity of an object, the point till which it resists bending. Rubber, elastic can be easily bent while wood or iron cannot be bent.

7. Compressibility

A LPG Cylinder

Compressibility means how much the volume of a material can be changed when pressure is applied on it. Since solids and liquids have a definite volume, therefore it is very difficult to compress them. However, gases can be easily compressed and are used in compressed forms in our houses as *LPG or cooking gas*.

8. Transparency

Glass Window (Transparency)

It is the property that determines how well a material lets light pass through it. Glass, water and air let light pass through them very easily.

Solids like wood, iron and steel do not let light pass through them. Materials that let light pass through them appear transparent, i.e., they appear to be colourless.

9. Viscosity

A River Flowing Smoothly

Viscosity or stickiness is the property which makes a liquid flow smoothly or slowly. If the viscosity is less, the liquid will flow freely and smoothly but if the viscosity is high, the liquid will flow slowly. Water has a low viscosity and flows smoothly while the lava from a volcano has a high viscosity.

Volcano has High Viscosity

10. Malleability

Malleability is the property of a solid. It determines how easily a solid can be shaped without breaking. The most common solid known for its malleability is gold. Different shapes, designs and patterns are made with gold and used as jewellery. This can happen only because gold is very malleable.

Gold is Malleable

Quick Facts

- **Substances, which break easily, are called brittle substances and substances, which can be beaten into sheets, are called malleable substances.**
- **Substances, which can be drawn into wires, are ductile substances.**
- **Substances that change their shape and size when an external force is applied and which regain their original form when the force is removed, are elastic substances.**
- **Substances, which absorb moisture from the air, are deliquescent. Substances that lose moisture are efflorescent.**
- **The process of intermixing of molecules is called diffusion.**
- **Opaque substances do not allow light to pass through. Transparent substances allow light to pass through. Translucent substances allow some light to pass through.**

Chapter - 3

CHANGING STATES OF MATTER

When solids get hot enough, *they melt and turn into liquids*. When liquids get cold enough, *they freeze and turn into solids*. When liquids become hot enough, they turn into steam or gas. At certain temperature, all substances change their states. *Gases* can be turned into *plasma* with the help of very cold temperature.

Matter changes its state through *melting, freezing, evaporation* and *condensation*. Heat is the most common way that changes the state of matter. Heat when applied to a solid changes it to a liquid. Heat changes a liquid to a gas. Heat is also involved in evaporating water from clothes that are hung out to dry. Condensation results in gases changing or converting into liquids.

Freezing

When liquids are put into cold temperature, their atoms become tightly packed together and they turn into solids. Water turns into ice when we keep it in the freezer. All liquids have different freezing points. If we keep both water and honey into the freezer, they will freeze at different temperatures.

Ice Cubes

Melting

When solids are heated, after a certain temperature, their atoms become loosely packed and they turn into liquids. Most solids have high melting points, therefore a large amount of heat is needed to melt them. In factories, iron is heated and melted to make different instruments with it.

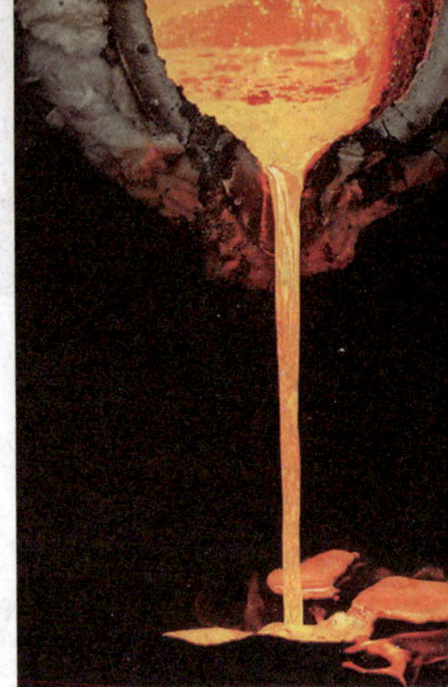

Motten Iron

Evaporation

When *we heat a liquid, it begins to evaporate*. Water evaporates in the form of steam. We can see this steam when we boil water in a pan in our houses. Another common example of evaporation is when we hang our clothes out in the sun to dry. The heat from the sun slowly evaporates all the water still present in our clothes and our clothes become dry.

Water Evaporating from Wet Clothes

Condensation

Condensation occurs when a gas comes in contact with a cool surface. The lower temperature changes the form of a gas into liquid. In summers, when we leave out a bottle of cold water, we can see water droplets being formed on its outside. This is the air around that is changing in liquid form because of the cold surface of bottle.

Plastic Bottles with Water Droplets on the Outside

Water exists in all three states on our planet. It is also one of the reasons that life exists on the earth. In liquid state, we use it as water for drinking, washing and various other purposes. In solid state, we use water as ice and in gaseous state, we use it as steam.

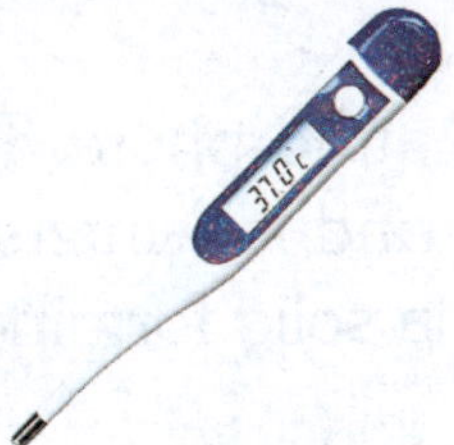

A Digital Thermometer

Do it Yourself

Take a few ice cubes from the freezer and put them in a pan on the stove. As it gets heated, the ice will change into liquid water. If you keep applying the heat, the water will begin to boil. As the water begins to boil, you will be able to see water vapours rising from the pan.

Ice Cubes

Now cover the pan with a plate. After some time, when you remove the plate, you will see water droplets on it which were formed because steam changed into water on touching the cooler plate. This water in liquid form can again be frozen by putting it in the freezer.

Boiling Water

Changing States of Water in Nature

It is fun and interesting to see the changing states of water because we can try it at home. But water also changes its state on a very large scale on the earth. Glaciers that melt in summers bring water to the rivers. The heat from the sun evaporates water from the rivers and the oceans into the

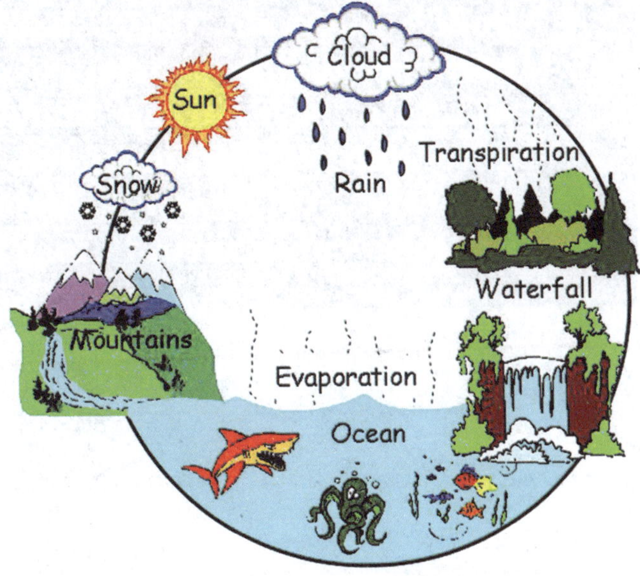

Water Cycle in Nature

atmosphere. Then when it rains, the water returns back to the earth and in winters, the water present on the mountains freezes back to a solid forming ice or snow.

Quick Facts

- Mercury is the only metal that exists in liquid form at room temperature. This is because its melting point is low. Mercury is most often used in thermometers to measure the body temperature.
- Stars, including the sun, are made of matter in the plasma state. In fact, most of the matter in the Universe, particularly in the Galaxy exists in the plasma state! The states of matter can also be called the phases of matter.
- The state of matter of a substance depends on how fast its particles move and how strong the attraction is between its atoms and molecules.
- Solids maintain their shapes and volume. The particles of the substance vibrate in place. The vibration isn't strong enough to overcome the attraction of the particles and cause them to separate. As a result, the forces between the particles cause them to lock together.

Chapter - 4

MASS, VOLUME AND DENSITY

Mass

Mass is the amount of matter an object has. It is measured in grams. *Mass is different from weight*. Mass measures the matter in an object, whereas weight is the measurement of the pull of gravity of an object. Mass is measured using a balance to compare the known amount of matter to the unknown amount of matter, whereas, weight is measured by a scale. The mass of an object does not change when the location of an object changes, but the weight of an object changes according to its location.

Volume

Volume is the amount of space an object occupies. The space can be occupied by any substance like solid, liquid or gas. The volume of an object is calculated by the amount of liquid displacement. *Volume is expressed in cubic centimetres*.

Density

The density of a material helps to distinguish it from other materials. Density is calculated by the formula: Density = Mass/Volume. Density is measured in mass per unit volume. Therefore, $D = \frac{M}{V}$

Every substance has a different density. Density is defined as the relative heaviness of an object with a constant volume. It also refers to how closely or tightly are the atoms of a substance packed. For example, Styrofoam and Stone both are solids, but they do not have the same density.

A Piece of Styrofoam

A Piece of Rock

Measuring Mass, Volume and Density

Mass

Mass is measured using a triple balance beam. It is called so because it has three beams that allow you to move known masses along the beam. It is unaffected by gravity and gives a true measure of the mass of an object.

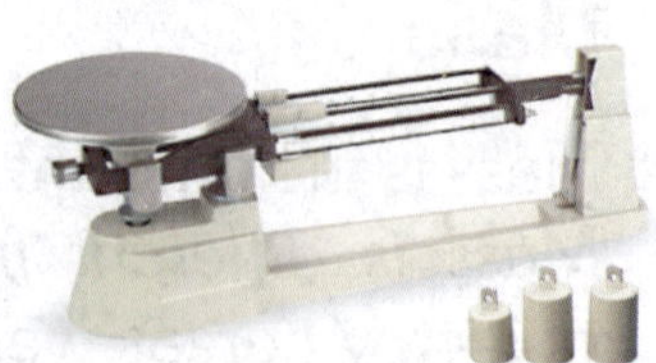
A Triple Balance Beam

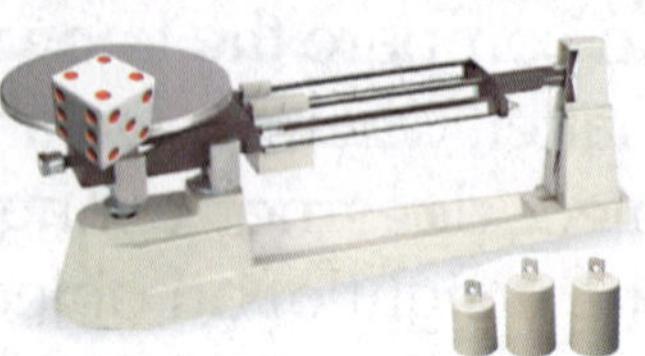
Weighing a Dice

There are many other types of balances. Scientists often use different types of balances to calculate a very small amount of mass.

Volume

There are two types of objects, *regular* and *irregular*. Regular objects have systematical dimensions, whereas, irregular objects have irregular dimensions. If you want to measure the volume of a regular object, it is simply length times height times weight. The formula is Volume = Length × Height × Weight (V = L×W×H) and is expressed in cubic centimetres.

The volume of irregular objects is measured by the displacement of a liquid. This is done in laboratories using a graduated cylinder.

Do it Yourself

Take a glass bowl and fill it half way. Mark the level of the water. Now take a small stone and put it inside the water. You will notice a rise in the water level. Mark the new level. The difference between both the levels is the volume of the stone. A graduated cylinder measures the volume of an irregular object in the same way. It has proper markings on its sides so that the measurement is accurate.

Glass Bowl with Stones in It

Density

As we read earlier, the formula for measuring density is Density = Mass/Volume. So for measuring the density of any object, you should first measure their mass and volume. Once you have both the quantities, you can find out the density using the above formula.

Quick Facts

- **Weightlessness can be felt when a person falls freely and suddenly. For example: The weight of an object comes from the fact that a person is supported by the floor or the chair, etc. If this support is removed, then the person falls freely and he feels weightlessness. Therefore, weightlessness refers to a state of being in a free fall in which there is no support.**
- **While on a roller coaster, if there is a sudden fall at high speed, then you can feel this weightlessness. This happens because suddenly all support is taken away and the person is almost falling freely.**

- **Objects with mass are attracted to each other, and towards the Earth's surface. This is known as gravity.**
- **Density measurements are used when weight and weight distribution are important. This may include the construction of ships, buildings, airplanes and other modes of transportation. Density measurements are also useful when determining how much force is required to move a liquid through piping or tubing. Density also comes into play when packaging engineers design squirt bottles for things such as ketchup and mustard.**

Chapter - 5

ATOMS

An atom is the smallest particle that makes up any matter. It is the smallest unit of an element that exhibits all the chemical properties of that element. It consists of a tiny, dense, central nucleus made up of *protons* and *neutrons* surrounded by *electrons*.

Some matter is made up of only one kind of atom. The properties of an element depend upon the kind of atoms that it is made up of. There are about *112 known kinds of atoms* and therefore, there are around *112 known elements*.

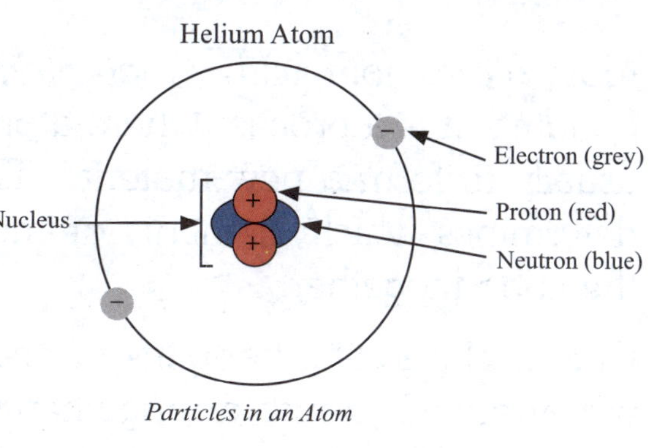

Particles in an Atom

There are three particles present in an atom: **Electrons** which have a **negative charge**, **Protons** which have a **positive charge** and **Neutrons** which have no charge.

Protons and Neutrons are present inside the **nucleus** of an atom. The nucleus is in the centre and contains all the mass of the atom. Electrons are present outside the nucleus. There are equal number of protons and electrons in an atom. Almost all the space inside an atom is empty and the kind of atom is determined by the number of protons in it. This is called the **atomic number**.

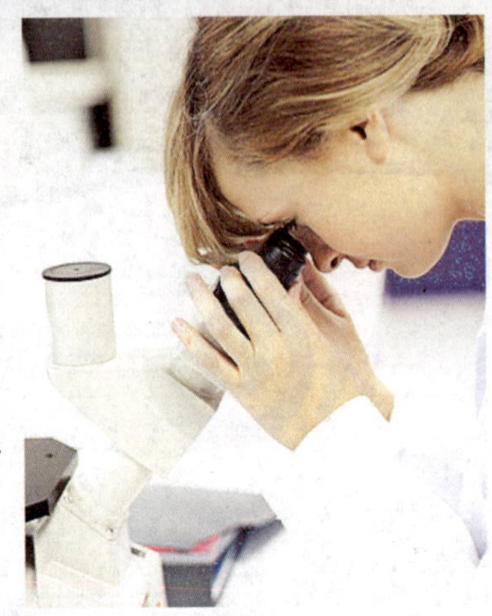

Scientist Observing through a Microscope

Atoms are very small and therefore, they cannot be seen through the naked eye. Powerful microscopes are required to know the structure of the atom. Earlier, there were no powerful microscopes, therefore scientists made models of the structure of the atom on paper to study them.

Now with the help of new technologies, scientists are finding more about the atom and the models of an atom keep changing. They may keep changing in the future too keeping in mind the advancement in technology.

Chemical Bonding

Most atoms join with other atoms, and this is called chemical bonding. It is a process where atoms and molecules bond together usually to form a new material. The outer electrons' orbit or shell determines which elements or molecules combine and how well they bond together.

Chemical bonding happens through the changes in how electrons are arranged. Some arrangements are stable and some are very unstable. When an atom bonds with another, it usually does so in a way to make the arrangement *stable*.

There are two ways in which chemical bonding happens: either atoms can transfer electrons from one to another or, they can share electrons. An atom can be stable only if there are equal number of protons and electrons in it. The two main types of bonds formed by atoms are:

1. Ionic Bond

An ionic bond is formed when one atom accepts or gives electrons to another atom. Ionic bonds are weaker than covalent bonds. Most of the solid things in the universe, like rocks, use ionic bonds to hold themselves together. *Ionic bonds are formed between metals and non-metals.*

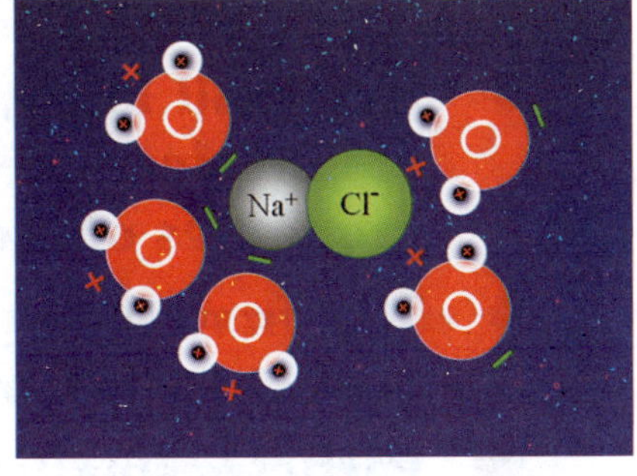

Bonding between $Na^+ + Cl^- = NaCl$ (Common Salt)

During the reaction of sodium and chlorine, sodium loses its one electron to chlorine which results in a positively charged sodium ion and negatively charged chlorine ion.

2. Covalent Bond

In covalent bonding, the atoms are unstable because their outer rings of electrons aren't filled up. When they share electrons with other atoms, these atoms fill up their outer rings and become stable.

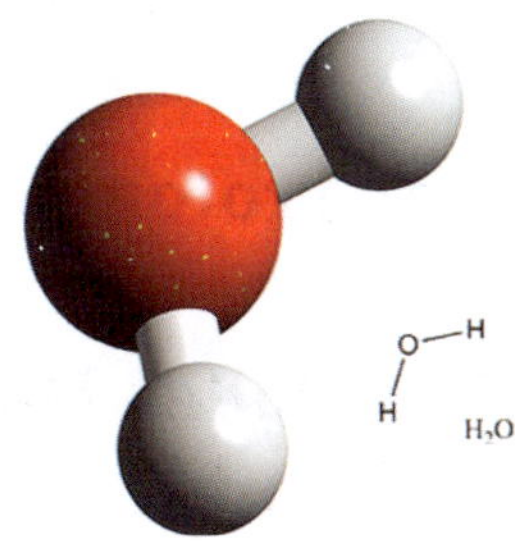

A Molecule of Water (H_2O)

In water, for example, the oxygen atom needs two more electrons to be stable and the hydrogen atoms, each need one. When they form a bond, the oxygen atom shares one electron with each of the hydrogen atoms, and the hydrogen atoms, each share one electron with the oxygen atom.

For every pair of electrons shared, a single covalent bond is formed. Some atoms share multiple pairs of electrons forming multiple covalent bonds.

Quick Facts

- As we all know, an Atom is the smallest particle of an element still having the same chemical properties of the element.
- The first theory of the atom's appearance was made in 1911 by Ernest Rutherford.
- Particles smaller than atoms are called subatomic particles. Electrons, protons and neutrons are the three major subatomic particles. Today scientists understand that protons and neutrons are made of even smaller particles called quarks which are tied together with particles called gluons.
- It is believed that an atom is made of 200 or more than 200 subatomic particles because it is believed that in an atom, there is so much space and electrons take only 1/1000th of the volume. This space may have some more subatomic particles in it.
- An atom can lose electrons, but not protons or neutrons.
- If you split a nuclear atom, it will explode! This fact led to the invention of the Atom Bomb!

Chapter - 6

MOLECULES

A molecule is made up of two or more atoms. *When atoms bond together, they form molecules.* Molecules cannot be seen by the naked eye but they can be seen through an *electron microscope.* Almost everything on the earth and other planets is made up of molecules. Also some of the dust in space is made up of molecules.

The shape of molecules and the way in which they pack together help to explain how different materials behave. The smallest kind of molecule that exists in space is two hydrogen atoms combined together or H_2O. Most of the molecules in space are hydrogen atoms. These combine with other kinds of atoms and form different materials.

CH_4 (Methane)

Two hydrogen atoms combined with one oxygen atom makes water molecule. Hydrogen combined with carbon makes hydrocarbon molecules. Molecules bond with other atoms by ionic and covalent bonding.

Molecules in Different States Melt and Solidify

Molecules are always moving around. When they get heated, they begin to move faster and further. When a solid heats up, its molecules move faster until they break free from each other and move separately. This turns the solid into a liquid.

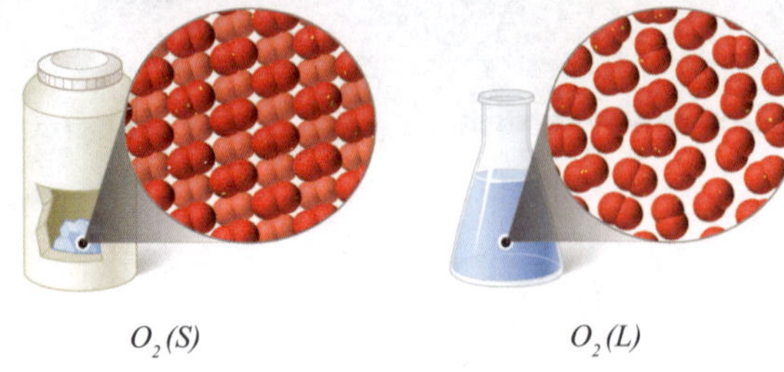

$O_2(S)$ $O_2(L)$

While, when a liquid cools, its molecules lose energy and become slow. They start sticking to each other, and turn the liquid into a solid.

Evaporate and Condense

Here O_2 = Oxygen (Element)
S = Solid G = Gas
L = Liquid

When a liquid heats up, its molecules start moving faster and further apart until they are moving so fast that they float as gas.

$O_2(L)$

$O_2(G)$

When a gas is cooled, its molecules lose energy and become slow. They then start sticking together and form a liquid.

Diamond and Graphite

Diamond is the hardest natural substance on the earth. Each atom in a diamond molecule is joined by strong bonds to four neighbouring atoms and this makes diamond very hard.

Diamond

Pencils with Graphite

Graphite is also a carbon atom like diamond but it is much softer than diamond. This is because the atoms in graphite are arranged in a different way which makes graphite soft. Each carbon atom in graphite is joined to three neighbouring atoms.

New Materials

The Planet, Earth

Molecules bond with each other in different ways and form new substances. New and different materials are being made by joining two or more molecules. The biggest organic molecule today is the DNA or the Deoxyribonucleic acid. Each molecule of DNA has more than two billion carbon atoms with other kinds of atoms.

Scientists today make new kinds of molecules in laboratories and factories. Some of the biggest molecules made by man are *plastics*. *Plastics are hydrocarbon molecules*. New molecules are also made in the field of medicine to find cures for diseases.

After the **Big Bang**, when the planets were taking form, most planets were being made of lighter materials. The earth being closer to the sun, was made from heavier molecules like iron. A lot of silicon and other minerals also piled on the earth and made up the rocks of the earth's crust.

Quick Facts

- **Molecules are made up of two or more atoms, either of the same element or of two or more different elements, joined by one or more covalent chemical bonds.**
- **A molecule is two or more atoms bonded together. It is normally the smallest bit of a substance that exists independently.**
- **According to the kinetic-molecular theory, the molecules of a substance are in constant motion. The state (solid, liquid, or gaseous) in which matter**

appears depends on the speed and separation of the molecules in the matter.

- Substances differ according to the structure and composition of their molecules. A molecular compound is represented by its molecular formula; for example, water is represented by the formula, H_2O. A more complex structural formula is sometimes used to show the arrangement of atoms in the molecule.
- The shape of a molecule depends on the arrangement of bonds that hold its atoms together.
- Ammonia or NH_3 molecules are pyramid shaped; some protein molecules are long spirals.
- Compounds only exist as molecules. If the atoms in the molecule of a compound were separated, the compound would cease to exist.
- Diamond is used to cut other hard substances in industries. It is the hardest substance known but it can be destroyed by burning.

Chapter - 7

ELEMENTS

Elements are the building blocks of all matter. When we talk about elements, we are referring to chemical elements. Everything from living things, plants to rocks are made up of elements. So far *117 elements have been discovered*, out of which *94 of them are found naturally*, while the others have been created by scientists in laboratories.

Everything around us is made up of elements in different combinations. The air around us is made up of mostly nitrogen and also elements like oxygen, carbon and a few others. We are made up of mostly *carbon, hydrogen, oxygen and nitrogen*.

Periodic Table

In the periodic table, *elements are arranged by the number of protons in their atoms*. The table looks like a grid and the elements are placed at specific places because of the way they look and act. The rows and columns in the periodic table mean a different thing.

One row in the periodic table is called a period. The elements in one row have something in common. All the elements in the first row have one *atomic orbital*. In the second row, two atomic orbitals

1A	2A	3B	4B	5B	6B	7B	8B	8B	8B	1B	2B	3A	4A	5A	6A	7A	8A
1 H 1.008																	2 He 4.003
3 Li 6.941	4 Be 9.012											5 B 10.81	6 C 12.01	7 N 14.01	8 O 16.00	9 F 19.00	10 Ne 20.18
11 Na 23.00	12 Mg 24.31											13 Al 26.98	14 Si 28.09	15 P 30.97	16 S 32.06	17 Cl 35.45	18 Ar 39.95
19 K 39.10	20 Ca 40.08	21 Sc 44.96	22 Ti 47.90	23 V 50.94	24 Cr 52.00	25 Mn 54.94	26 Fe 55.85	27 Co 58.93	28 Ni 58.70	29 Cu 63.55	30 Zn 65.38	31 Ga 69.72	32 Ge 72.59	33 As 74.92	34 Se 78.96	35 Br 79.90	36 Kr 83.80
37 Rb 85.47	38 Sr 87.62	39 Y 88.91	40 Zr 91.22	41 Nb 92.91	42 Mo 95.94	43 Tc (98)	44 Ru 101.1	45 Rh 102.9	46 Pd 106.4	47 Ag 107.9	48 Cd 112.4	49 In 114.8	50 Sn 118.7	51 Sb 121.8	52 Te 127.6	53 I 126.9	54 Xe 131.3
55 Cs 132.9	56 Ba 137.3	57 La 138.9	72 Hf 178.5	73 Ta 180.9	74 W 183.9	75 Re 186.2	76 Os 190.2	77 Ir 192.2	78 Pt 195.1	79 Au 197.0	80 Hg 200.6	81 Tl 204.4	82 Pb 207.2	83 Bi 209.0	84 Po (209)	85 At (210)	86 Rn (222)
87 Fr (223)	88 Ra 226.0	89 Ac 227.0	104 Rf (261)	105 Ha (262)	106 Unh (263)	107 Uns (262)		109 Une (267)									

Lanthanides	58 Ce 140.1	59 Pr 140.9	60 Nd 144.2	61 Pm (145)	62 Sm 150.4	63 Eu 152.0	64 Gd 157.3	65 Tb 158.9	66 Dy 162.5	67 Ho 164.9	68 Er 167.3	69 Tm 168.9	70 Yb 173.0	71 Lu 175.0
Actinides	90 Th 232.0	91 Pa 231.0	92 U 238.0	93 Np 237.0	94 Pu (244)	95 Am (243)	96 Cm (247)	97 Bk (247)	98 Cf (251)	99 Es (252)	100 Fm (257)	101 Md (258)	102 No (259)	103 Lr (260)

The Periodic Table

and so on. *The maximum number of atomic orbitals for an element is seven.*

One column of the periodic table is called a group. All the elements in the same group have the same number of electrons in their outer orbital. All elements in the first group have one electron in the outer orbital. Elements in the second group have two electrons in their outer orbital and so on.

The periodic table arranges elements into a pattern so that you can predict their properties based on where they are located in the periodic table.

Metals and Non-Metals

Metals

Most elements are metals. *Metals are separated from non-metals*

in the periodic table with a zig-zag line. The properties of metals are: All metals are shiny, and they are good conductors of heat and electricity. They have a high melting point and a high density, and they are malleable and ductile. They are usually solids at room temperature (the exception is mercury). They are opaque and sonorous, i.e., they make a bell like sound when struck.

Metals

Non-Metals

Non-metals have the following properties: They do not shine, and they are poor conductors of heat and electricity. They are non-ductile and brittle, may be solid, liquid or gas at room temperature, and they are transparent and are not sonorous.

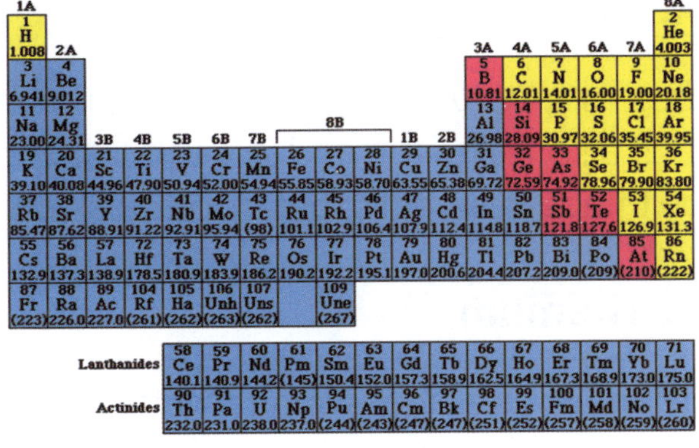

1A	2A	3B	4B	5B	6B	7B	8B			1B	2B	3A	4A	5A	6A	7A	8A
1 H 1.008																	2 He 4.003
3 Li 6.941	4 Be 9.012											5 B 10.81	6 C 12.01	7 N 14.01	8 O 16.00	9 F 19.00	10 Ne 20.18
11 Na 23.00	12 Mg 24.31											13 Al 26.98	14 Si 28.09	15 P 30.97	16 S 32.06	17 Cl 35.45	18 Ar 39.95
19 K 39.10	20 Ca 40.08	21 Sc 44.96	22 Ti 47.90	23 V 50.94	24 Cr 52.00	25 Mn 54.94	26 Fe 55.85	27 Co 58.93	28 Ni 58.70	29 Cu 63.55	30 Zn 65.38	31 Ga 69.72	32 Ge 72.59	33 As 74.92	34 Se 78.96	35 Br 79.90	36 Kr 83.80
37 Rb 85.47	38 Sr 87.62	39 Y 88.91	40 Zr 91.22	41 Nb 92.91	42 Mo 95.94	43 Tc (98)	44 Ru 101.1	45 Rh 102.9	46 Pd 106.4	47 Ag 107.9	48 Cd 112.4	49 In 114.8	50 Sn 118.7	51 Sb 121.8	52 Te 127.6	53 I 126.9	54 Xe 131.3
55 Cs 132.9	56 Ba 137.3	57 La 138.9	72 Hf 178.5	73 Ta 180.9	74 W 183.9	75 Re 186.2	76 Os 190.2	77 Ir 192.2	78 Pt 195.1	79 Au 197.0	80 Hg 200.6	81 Tl 204.4	82 Pb 207.2	83 Bi 209.0	84 Po (209)	85 At (210)	86 Rn (222)
87 Fr (223)	88 Ra 226.0	89 Ac 227.0	104 Rf (261)	105 Ha (262)	106 Unh (263)	107 Uns (262)		109 Une (267)									

Lanthanides	58 Ce 140.1	59 Pr 140.9	60 Nd 144.2	61 Pm (145)	62 Sm 150.4	63 Eu 152.0	64 Gd 157.3	65 Tb 158.9	66 Dy 162.5	67 Ho 164.9	68 Er 167.3	69 Tm 168.9	70 Yb 173.0	71 Lu 175.0
Actinides	90 Th 232.0	91 Pa 231.0	92 U 238.0	93 Np 237.0	94 Pu (244)	95 Am (243)	96 Cm (247)	97 Bk (247)	98 Cf (251)	99 Es (252)	100 Fm (257)	101 Md (258)	102 No (259)	103 Lr (260)

Non-Metals

Uses of Elements

We use a lot of metals in our daily lives. Some metals are also used for specific purposes in laboratories and factories. Elements are used for various useful as well as decorative purposes.

1. Gold

Gold is a precious metal used to make jewellery.

Gold Jewellery

2. Copper

Copper is a good conductor of electricity and is used to make electrical wires.

Electrical Copper Wires

3. Mercury

Mercury is a liquid metal. It is used in dental fillings and in thermometers.

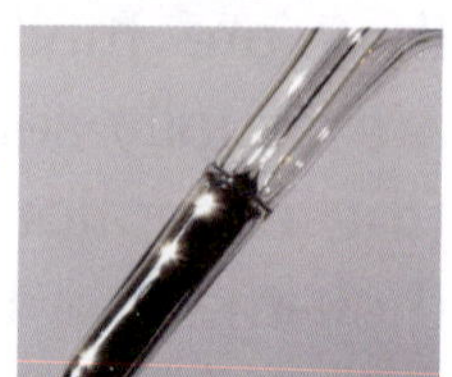
A Mercury Thermometer

4. Iron

Iron is a very strong element. It has many uses. It is also magnetic and is used to make a variety of things from grills, gates to trucks and magnets.

A Grilled Gate

5. Titanium

Titanium is a light-weight metal and it is used in the manufacturing of aeroplanes.

Titanium in Aeroplanes

6. Helium

Helium is a gas used in balloons which makes them float in air because they are lighter than air.

Helium Gas Balloons

7. Chlorine

Chlorine is a *yellow-green gas*. It is used as a *bleach* and also to make *plastics*.

Chlorine Bleach

8. Silicon

Silicon Computer Chip

Silicon is a non-metal used to make computers and computer chips.

9. Sulphur

Sulphur Particles

Sulphur is a *yellow non-metal*. It is used to harden rubber to make tyres.

10. Aluminium

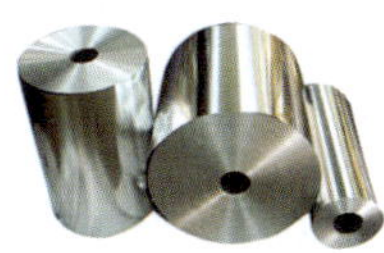
Aluminium Rods

Aluminium is a *soft shiny metal*. It is used to make a number of useful things like aluminium foils, roofs, soft drink cans, aeroplanes, etc.

Quick Facts

- **Each chemical element on the Periodic Table is arranged according to its atomic number, as based on the periodic law, so that chemical elements with similar properties are in the same column.**
- **The Periodic Table is simple to use - just look at the symbols for the elements of your choice for additional facts and information, and for an instant comparison of the Atomic Weights, Melting Points, Boiling Points and Mass of a specific element with any other of the elements.**
- **Nitrogen is the most abundantly found element in the atmosphere. It composes 78 percent of the atmosphere at the ground level, Oxygen comprises about 21 percent and the rest 1 percent consists of all other gases.**

Chapter - 8

PROPERTIES OF ELEMENTS

The properties of elements are classified as either **chemical** or **physical**. Chemical properties are observed through a chemical reaction and physical properties are observed by examining a pure sample of the element.

The chemical properties of an element are due to the distribution of electrons that are involved in chemical reactions. A chemical reaction does not affect atomic nucleus, therefore the atomic number remains the same.

The physical properties of elements can be observed in the collection of atoms and molecules of an element. These include its colour, density, melting point, boiling point, thermal and electrical conductivity, etc.

Elements are grouped in the periodic table according to their properties. The major classification between elements is metals, non-metals and metalloids. Elements that have very similar properties are referred to as **families**. Some families of elements are *halogens*, *inert gases* and *alkali metals*.

Metals, Non-Metals and Metalloids

Metals have properties that you normally associate with a metal in your daily life. Most elements are metals.

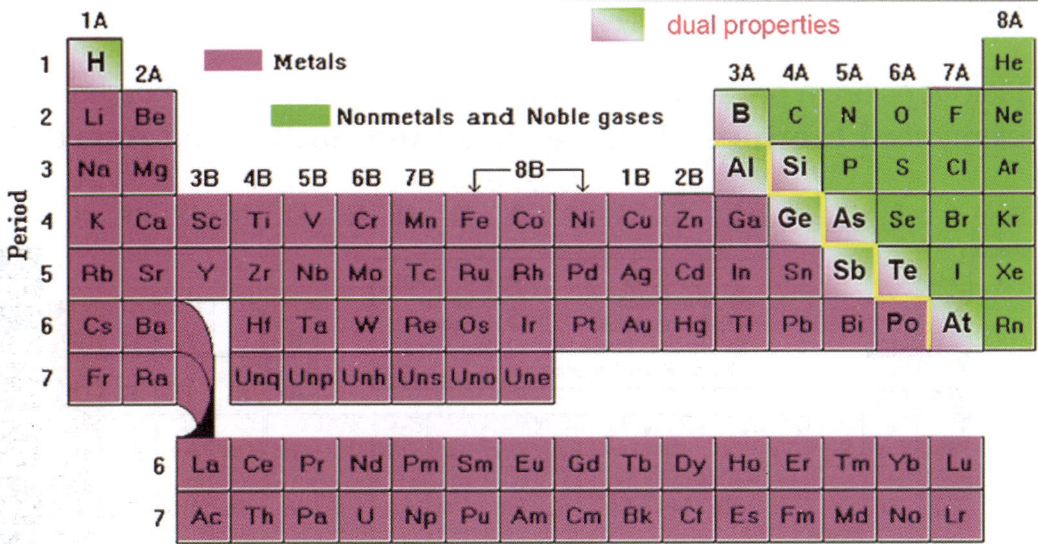

Non-metals have properties opposite to those of metals.

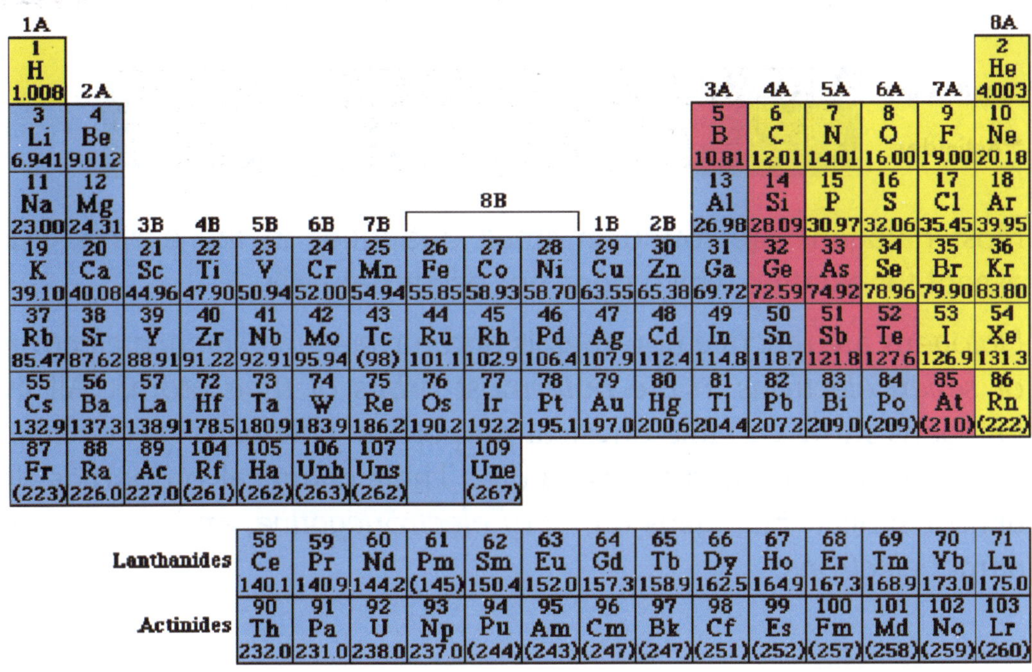

The Periodic Table

Metalloids have properties of both metals and non-metals.

Halogens

Halogens are a particular type of non-metals. There are *five halogen elements:* **Fluorine, Chlorine, Bromine, Iodine** and **Astatine**.

Period \ Group	1	2	3	4	5	6	7	8	9	10	11	12	13	14	15	16	17	18
1	1 H																	2 He
2	3 Li	4 Be											5 B	6 C	7 N	8 O	9 F	10 Ne
3	11 Na	12 Mg											13 Al	14 Si	15 P	16 S	17 Cl	18 Ar
4	19 K	20 Ca	21 Sc	22 Ti	23 V	24 Cr	25 Mn	26 Fe	27 Co	28 Ni	29 Cu	30 Zn	31 Ga	32 Ge	33 As	34 Se	35 Br	36 Kr
5	37 Rb	38 Sr	39 Y	40 Zr	41 Nb	42 Mo	43 Tc	44 Ru	45 Rh	46 Pd	47 Ag	48 Cd	49 In	50 Sn	51 Sb	52 Te	53 I	54 Xe
6	55 Cs	56 Ba	57* La	72 Hf	73 Ta	74 W	75 Re	76 Os	77 Ir	78 Pt	79 Au	80 Hg	81 Tl	82 Pb	83 Bi	84 Po	85 At	86 Rn
7	87 Fr	88 Ra	89** Ac	104 Rf	105 Db	106 Sg	107 Bh	108 Hs	109 Mt	110 Ds	111 Rg	112 Cn	113 Uut	114 Uuq	115 Uup	116 Uuh	117 Uus	118 Uuo

- Non Metals
- Alkali Metals
- Alkaline Metals
- Transition Metals
- Rare Earth Elements
- Noble Gases
- Metalloids
- Halogens
- Other Metals

*Lanthanides	58 Ce	59 Pr	60 Nd	61 Pm	62 Sm	63 Eu	64 Gd	65 Tb	66 Dy	67 Ho	68 Er	69 Tm	70 Yb	71 Lu
**Actinides	90 Th	91 Pa	92 U	93 Np	94 Pu	95 Am	96 Cm	97 Bk	98 Cf	99 Es	100 Fm	101 Md	102 No	103 Lr

Most halogens are found in small quantities in the earth's crust except for astatine which does not occur naturally.

Halogens are reactive non-metals and have *seven valence electrons or seven electrons in the outermost orbits of their atoms*. All the halogens show variable physical properties. Halogens can be *solid, liquid or gas* at room temperature. Their chemical properties are almost similar. Halogens are very *electronegative*, and *their atoms attract electrons*.

Inert Gases

Inert gases are also called noble gases because they hardly react with other chemicals. The inert gases are *helium, neon, argon, krypton, xenon and radon*.

Periodic Table of the Elements

© www.elementsdatabase.com

- hydrogen
- alkali metals
- alkali earth metals
- transition metals
- poor metals
- nonmetals
- noble gases
- rare earth metals

1	2	3	4	5	6	7	8	9	10	11	12	13	14	15	16	17	18
H 1																	He 2
Li 3	Be 4											B 5	C 6	N 7	O 8	F 9	Ne 10
Na 11	Mg 12											Al 13	Si 14	P 15	S 16	Cl 17	Ar 18
K 19	Ca 20	Sc 21	Ti 22	V 23	Cr 24	Mn 25	Fe 26	Co 27	Ni 28	Cu 29	Zn 30	Ga 31	Ge 32	As 33	Se 34	Br 35	Kr 36
Rb 37	Sr 38	Y 39	Zr 40	Nb 41	Mo 42	Tc 43	Ru 44	Rh 45	Pd 46	Ag 47	Cd 48	In 49	Sn 50	Sb 51	Te 52	I 53	Xe 54
Cs 55	Ba 56	La 57	Hf 72	Ta 73	W 74	Re 75	Os 76	Ir 77	Pt 78	Au 79	Hg 80	Tl 81	Pb 82	Bi 83	Po 84	At 85	Rn 86
Fr 87	Ra 88	Ac 89	Unq 104	Unp 105	Unh 106	Uns 107	Uno 108	Une 109	Unn 110								

Ce 58	Pr 59	Nd 60	Pm 61	Sm 62	Eu 63	Gd 64	Tb 65	Dy 66	Ho 67	Er 68	Tm 69	Yb 70	Lu 71
Th 90	Pa 91	U 92	Np 93	Pu 94	Am 95	Cm 96	Bk 97	Cf 98	Es 99	Fm 100	Md 101	No 102	Lr 103

Inert gases are used by us in many ways. Neon is used in *advertising signs*, and argon is used in *light bulbs*. Helium is used in balloons and to cool things, and xenon is used in *headlights* of new cars. The inert gases are rare in nature, but they are useful too.

Alkali Metals

Metals, such as *lithium, sodium, potassium, rubidium, cesium and francium* are called Alkali Metals. They exhibit some of the properties

Periodic Table of the Elements

- hydrogen
- alkali metals
- alkali earth metals
- transition metals
- poor metals
- nonmetals
- noble gases
- rare earth metals

1	2	3	4	5	6	7	8	9	10	11	12	13	14	15	16	17	18
H 1																	He 2
Li 3	Be 4											B 5	C 6	N 7	O 8	F 9	Ne 10
Na 11	Mg 12											Al 13	Si 14	P 15	S 16	Cl 17	Ar 18
K 19	Ca 20	Sc 21	Ti 22	V 23	Cr 24	Mn 25	Fe 26	Co 27	Ni 28	Cu 29	Zn 30	Ga 31	Ge 32	As 33	Se 34	Br 35	Kr 36
Rb 37	Sr 38	Y 39	Zr 40	Nb 41	Mo 42	Tc 43	Ru 44	Rh 45	Pd 46	Ag 47	Cd 48	In 49	Sn 50	Sb 51	Te 52	I 53	Xe 54
Cs 55	Ba 56	La 57	Hf 72	Ta 73	W 74	Re 75	Os 76	Ir 77	Pt 78	Au 79	Hg 80	Ti 81	Pb 82	Bi 83	Po 84	At 85	Rn 86
Fr 87	Ra 88	Ac 89	Unq 104	Unp 105	Unh 106	Uns 107	Uno 108	Une 109	Unn 110								

Ce 58	Pr 59	Nd 60	Pm 61	Sm 62	Eu 63	Gd 64	Tb 65	Dy 66	Ho 67	Er 68	Tm 69	Yb 70	Lu 71
Th 90	Pa 91	U 92	Np 93	Pu 94	Am 95	Cm 96	Bk 97	Cf 98	Es 99	Fm 100	Md 101	No 102	Lr 103

of metals, but their densities are lower than normal metals. Alkali metals have one electron that is loosely bound. They have low *ionization energy and low electronegativity*. They are highly reactive to other chemicals.

Transition Elements

Transition elements possess most of the properties of normal metals and are therefore called *transition metals*. These elements are very hard and have *high melting* and *boiling points*. They are *good conductors of electricity* and are *malleable*. They have *low ionization energies*.

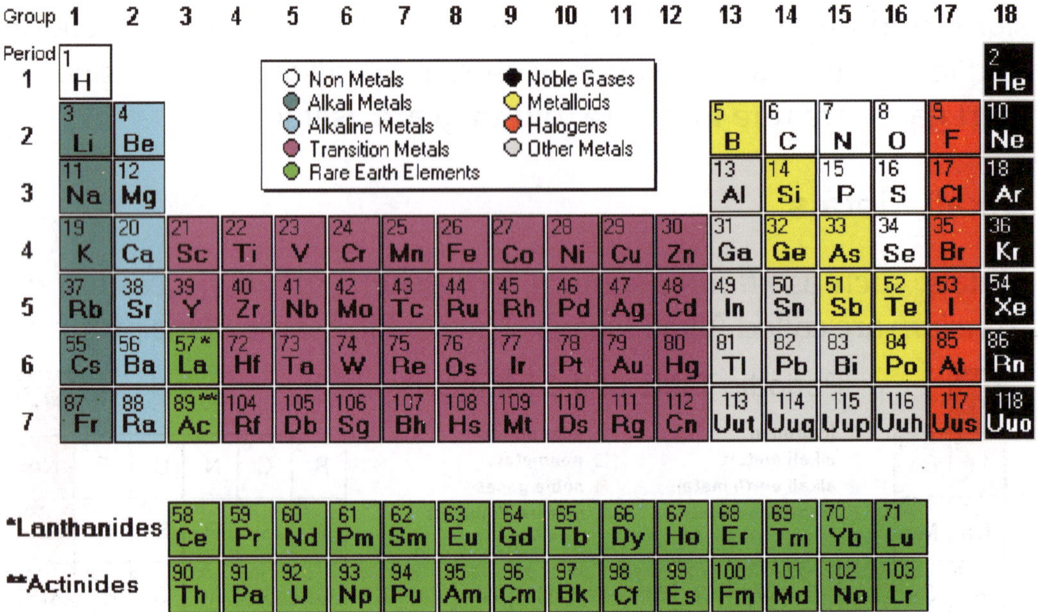

Quick Facts

- Any pure substance or element, under appropriate conditions, can exist in three different states: solids, liquids and gases. States of matter are examples of physical properties of a substance. Other physical properties include appearance (shiny, dull, smooth, rough), odour, electrical conductivity, thermal conductivity, hardness and density, etc.
- Physical changes are changes in outward appearances that do not alter chemical nature of the substance and produce no new substance. When a chemical change occurs, a new substance is produced. Just like physical properties describe the appearance or intensive properties of a substance, chemical properties describe the set of chemical changes that are possible for that substance or element to form new substances.
- However, the law of mass conservation (conservation of mass) simply states, that there is no detectable change in the total mass of materials when they react chemically (undergo a chemical change) to form new substances.

Chapter - 9

COMPOUNDS AND MIXTURES

When different elements bond together through a chemical reaction, they form **compounds**. Mixtures are formed when elements are mixed together and no bonding takes place.

Compounds

Compounds are chemical unions of separate elements. It is formed when different elements combine together in fixed proportions. The elements do not retain their properties and it is very difficult to separate the elements in a compound.

Water (H_2O) is a Compound

Common Salt (NaCl) is a Compound

Energy is given off or absorbed when a compound is formed and to separate its ingredients also, energy is needed. The creation of a compound depends on a chemical reaction.

Examples of compounds are **pure water (H_2O)**, which is a compound of *oxygen and hydrogen in a fixed proportion*, and **table salt (NaCl)**, which is a *compound of sodium and chlorine*.

Blast Furnace

Iron oxide (FeO) is a compound of iron and oxygen. To get pure iron, these elements have to be separated and this is done in a blast furnace. Extremely hot air is blasted into the furnace which makes the iron melt. The pure melted iron called the *pig iron* settles at the bottom. Pig iron is transformed into many useful forms of iron.

TYPES OF COMPOUNDS

Ionic Compounds

Ionic compounds are formed when metallic elements from the left side of the periodic table react with the non-metallic elements of the right side of the periodic table. These compounds have high boiling and melting points.

Ionic compounds are generally soluble in water, they are brittle and do not conduct electricity, although in the liquid form, they do conduct electricity.

Molecular Compounds

Molecular compounds are formed when two or more non-metals bond together and form molecules. These generally have low melting and boiling points. Molecular compounds do not conduct electricity in solid or liquid form. Some dissolve in water and some do not.

Mixtures

A mixture is formed when two or more materials join together, where no chemical reaction takes place and no chemical bonding occurs.

The components of a mixture retain their original properties and can be separated through physical means.

When a mixture is formed, no energy is either absorbed or given off. Mixtures can be created by mechanical means. Mixtures can be separated through the process of evaporation, filtering or the use of a magnetic force.

Examples of mixtures are air, which is a mixture of many gases, and sea water, which is a mixture of salt and water.

TYPES OF MIXTURES

Solution

Solutions are mixtures that are mixed in even distribution. A simple solution comprises two substances that are going to be combined. These are called the **solvent** and the **solute**. A solute is the substance to be dissolved and the solvent is the substance that is doing the dissolving. *Example: Sugar and water, here solute is sugar and the solvent is water.*

Dissolving of Sugar in Water

Suspension

Suspensions are a mixture of two substances, where they do not dissolve completely. The heavier component will settle down if the mixture is left undisturbed or by filtration. The components can be evenly distributed by shaking the mixture, but the solid will ultimately settle down. *Examples of suspensions are sand and water or oil and water.*

Quick Facts

- The composition of a mixture is variable. Each of its components retains its characteristic properties. Its components are easily separated. The relative proportions of the elements in a compound are fixed.
- However, the components of a compound do not retain their individual properties. For example, in table salt or common salt, both sodium and chlorine are poisonous; but their compound, table salt (NaCl) is absolutely essential to life and adds taste to our food. It takes large inputs of energy to separate the components of a compound.

Chapter - 10

REACTIONS AND CHANGES

When in a molecule, the atoms rearrange to form new kinds of molecules, change takes place. There are two types of changes that can happen: *Physical change and Chemical change*.

Chemical Change

A chemical change happens due to a chemical reaction, when chemicals combine in different ways to make new chemicals. Chemical changes take place at the molecular level and produce a new substance. The new substance is different from the original substances that were involved in the change.

Rusting of Iron

Chemical changes can result in molecules combining with each other to form larger molecules or molecules breaking apart to form smaller molecules. The basic structures of the molecules change. The rate of change may vary however.

Chemical changes can take a long time to happen or may happen in a few minutes. Rusting of iron takes a long time, while cooking creates chemical reactions in minutes.

Examples of chemical change are burning, cooking, rusting, etc.

Do it Yourself

You can do a chemical reaction by yourself at home. Put some vinegar in a bowl and add baking soda into it. This creates bubbles and fizz. You can make your own volcano by using these ingredients.

Vinegar and Baking Soda

Physical Change

A physical change does not create a new substance. It may change the size, shape or colour of a substance, but does not change its composition.

A Crushed Can

Melting, freezing, condensation, vaporization, etc. are all physical changes that result in the change of the state of the substance.

Broken Bangles

The materials involved in a physical change remain the same, even though they make look different after the change takes place. Physical changes do not affect the atomic and molecular structure of a substance. The core properties of substances do not change because physical changes do not affect them.

Snow Melting to form River

Examples of physical change are crushing of a tin can, melting of ice, stretching rubber band and breaking of glass.

Do it Yourself

We do a lot of physical changes everyday. When we cut a piece of paper, it is a physical change because the shape of the paper changes. When we boil water, it is a physical change as the state of water changes. When we add turmeric into water, the colour of water changes. Therefore, this also is a physical change.

Boiling of Water

Physical Change in Humans

Humans also go through a lot of physical changes during the course of life. We grow in height, lose our teeth, cut our hair and nails, colour our hair, etc — all these are physical changes that happen in our life.

Growth in Humans

Quick Facts

- **The earth also goes through physical changes. The mountains and glaciers move changes their shapes or formations. The river water and oceans rising are also instances of physical change. Hence, Drought and floods both are effects of physical change.**
- **Chemical changes take place on the molecular level. A chemical change produces a new substance. Examples of chemical changes include combustion (burning), cooking an egg, rusting of**

an iron pan, and mixing hydrochloric acid and sodium hydroxide to make salt and water.

- Physical changes are concerned with energy and states of matter. A physical change does not produce a new substance. Changes in state or phase (melting, freezing, vaporization, condensation, sublimation) are physical changes. Examples of physical changes include crushing a can, melting an ice cube, and breaking a bottle.
- A chemical change makes a substance that wasn't there before. There may be clues that a chemical reaction took place, such as light, heat, colour change, gas production, odour, or sound. The starting and ending materials of a physical change are the same, even though they may look different.

Chapter - 11

IRREVERSIBLE AND REVERSIBLE CHANGES

When two substances react and change and cannot be changed back to their original components, that is called an *irreversible change*. When two substances can be brought back to their original components after a change, it is called a *reversible change*.

Certain physical changes are reversible, but not all. While most chemical changes are irreversible because they produce a new substance and you cannot get back the original components after the change has occurred.

Irreversible Physical Changes

Do it Yourself

Take a bowl and mix flour and water in it. When we knead dough, it is a physical change because the basic components of both the ingredients, water and flour, remain the same. There is no chemical reaction and thus, no new component is formed.

A Bowl with Kneaded Dough

But you cannot reverse the change and get back flour and water as two separate ingredients. That is why this is an irreversible change.

Some physical changes cannot be reversed. Examples of physical changes that are irreversible are growing up, cooking, burning, rotting of food, etc.

Reversible Physical Change

Some physical changes are reversible. Though you need a method to get back the original ingredients, but it can be done.

Do it Yourself

Take a glass of water and mix some sand in it. The water will turn brownish and a physical change takes place. But if you let the solution stable and untouched for some time, you will notice the sand settling down. Left for a long time, you will notice that a large amount of sand has settled down and the water looks relatively cleaner.

Sand and Water

Now pick the glass slowly and pour the water into another glass leaving the sand behind. This way you have reversed a physical change. You have both the ingredients, water and sand, back and the change has been reversed.

Examples of reversible physical changes are separating salt from water through evaporation, bending a plastic and then straightening it, folding a piece of paper and then unfolding it, etc.

Irreversible Chemical Changes

Chemical changes cannot be reversed. As chemical changes occur at the molecular level, it is almost impossible to reverse them. A new substance in formed through a chemical change and the original components lose their properties.

Many new substances are produced in factories and laboratories using different elements. Substances, such as nylon, polymer, plastic, tin, steel — all are made with the help of chemical reactions. These new substances are better than their ingredients and are used for many purposes.

The most common irreversible chemical change that happens in our surroundings is rusting. Rusting happens when iron is exposed to oxygen for a long time. Iron oxide (FeO) is formed by a chemical reaction which is reddish-brown in colour.

Do It Yourself

Take a piece of iron that has rust on it. Rub it with a sand paper. You will notice that the rust is coming off, but iron is not restored to its original form. Once iron rusts, it becomes weak and loses its properties.

Rusted Iron Rods

Reversible Chemical Change

A reversible chemical change is turning water back into hydrogen and oxygen. This is done through the process of **electrolysis**. Water molecules are formed by bonding of two hydrogen and one oxygen atoms. These atoms can be separated by the process of electrolysis.

In this process, electricity is used to break apart water at the molecular level. Electricity is passed through some water between two electrodes placed in the water. This process separates hydrogen and oxygen and you can get the ingredients of water separately.

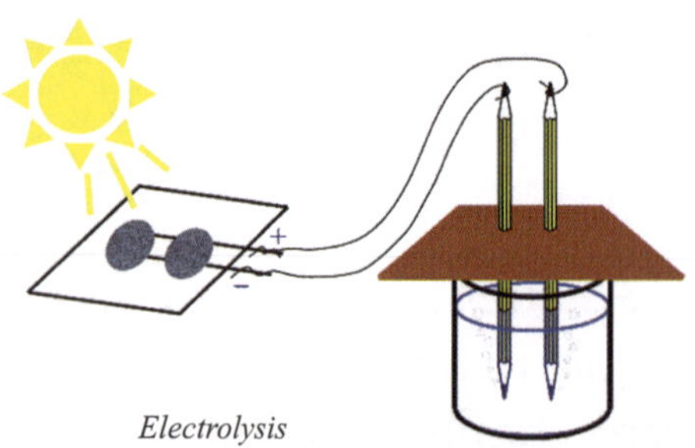

Electrolysis

The process of electrolysis is used to separate hydrogen and it is used as a **fuel**. This process was first formulated by **Michael Faraday** in **1820**.

Quick Facts

- **Many elements and some compounds change from solids to liquids and from liquids to gases when heated and the reverse when cooled. Some substances, such as iodine and carbon dioxide go directly from solid to gas in a process called sublimation.**
- **Ferro magnetic materials can become magnetic. The process is reversible and does not affect the chemical composition.**
- **Crystals in metals have a major effect on the physical properties of the metal including strength and ductility. The crystal type, shape and size can be altered by physical hammering, rolling and by heat.**
- **Most solutions of salts and some compounds, such as sugars can be separated by evaporation. Others, such as mixtures or volatile liquids, such as low molecular weight alcohols, can be separated by fractional distillation.**

Chapter - 12

ACIDS AND BASES

Every liquid that we see has either acidic or basic traits. One exception is distilled water. Water is neither acidic nor basic. The positive and negative ions in water are equal and cancel each other out. The ions in a solution make it *acidic or basic*.

A **pH scale** is used to measure how acidic or basic a solution is. The pH scale focuses on how many hydrogen ions and hydroxide ions are there in the solution. This scale goes from 0-14 with distilled water right in the middle, having its pH as 7.

Litmus Paper Test for Acids

Bases have a pH from 7-14 and acids have a pH from 0-7. Most liquids we see generally have a pH near 7. But in laboratories, you can find acids and bases that have high and low pH levels.

Acid

A solution that has an excess of H+ ions is an acid. An acid can be strong having a pH of 0-4 or weak having a pH of 3-6.

Properties of Acids

1. Acids taste sour. The word, acid comes from the Latin word, acere, which means sour.
2. Acids create hydrogen gas when they react with certain metal.
3. Acids react with bases to form salt and water.
4. Acids in an aqueous solution conduct electricity.
5. Acids change litmus from blue to red.

Examples of common acids are *citric acids* found in some *fruits* and *vegetables, vinegar, carbonic acid* and *lactic acid.*

Base

A solution that has an excess of OH+ ions is a base. A strong base has a very high pH from 10-14 and a weak base has a low pH from 8-10.

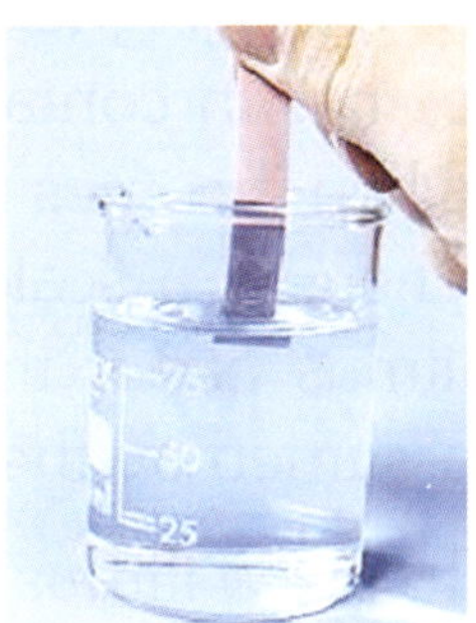

Litmus Paper Test in a Basic Solution

Properties of Bases

1. Bases taste bitter.
2. Bases feel slippery or soapy to touch.
3. Bases react with acids to form salts and water.
4. Bases in an aqueous solution conduct an electric current.
5. Bases don't change the colour of litmus. They can however change the acidic litmus, red, back to blue.

Detergent Powder Soap

Some common bases are *detergents, soaps, household ammonia,* etc.

pH Levels

The pH is the measure of concentration of hydrogen ions in a solution. There are certain substances that change colour when they come in contact with an acid or a base. These substances are called *pH indicators*. Generally to determine the pH, paper soaked in certain pH indicators is used.

Litmus Paper

Litmus is a substance obtained from lichens, a fungus. It has a property of changing its colour to blue when it comes in contact with a base and red when it comes in contact with an acid. There is a scale on the packet of the litmus paper that indicates the colour assumed by the paper as a function of the pH.

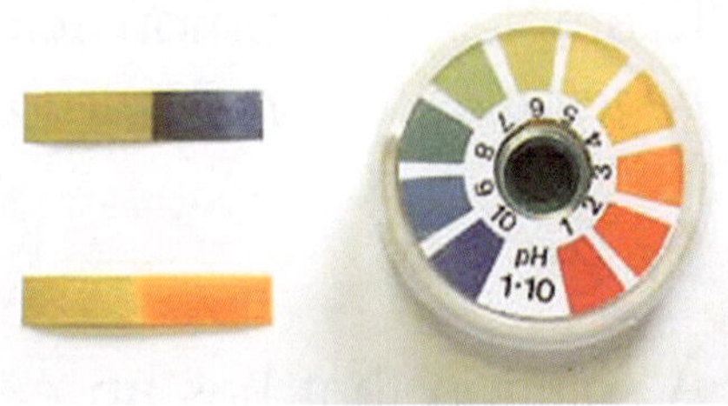

Litmus Papers and the Scales in them

To use a litmus paper, you have to dip one end of it into a solution and remove it immediately. The pH of the solution is determined by comparing its colour to the scale given on the packet.

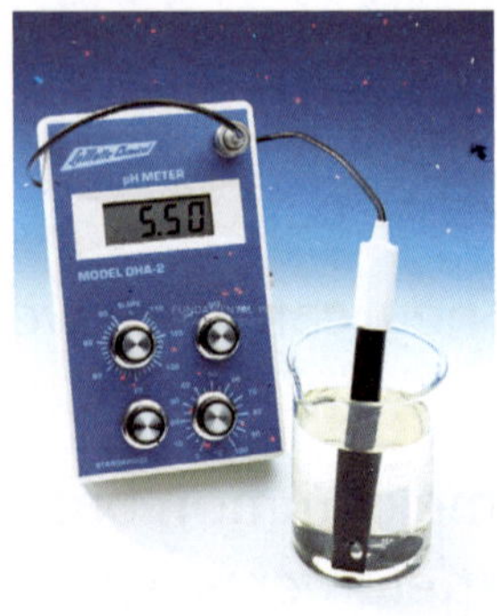

A pH Meter in Solution

pH Meter

A pH meter is an electronic instrument. It has a bulb which is sensitive to the presence of hydrogen ions in a solution. It has an analog meter to determine the pH of a solution. These instruments are more precise and convenient to use.

Aqueous and Neutral Solutions

An aqueous solution is mainly water. A neutral solution is one that has a pH of 7. *It is neither acidic nor basic.*

Do it Yourself

Check the pH of different solutions found in your home. Take different bowls and put lemon juice, water, vinegar, soft drink and detergent mixed with water in them. Use a litmus paper to determine whether these solutions are acidic, basic or neutral.

Lemons

Detergent Powder

Vinegar

Soft Drink

Quick Facts

- **Citric acid is present in many fruits such as lemon, orange, pineapple, etc. These fruits are also called citrus fruits.**
- **An Acid Rain is the combination of sulphur dioxide and nitrogen dioxide from polluting clouds, from nuclear reactor and other fossil fuels. This then combines with oxygen and water and forms the rain clouds which consist of nitric acid and sulphuric acid.**

Chapter - 13

SOLIDS

Solids are mostly hard because their molecules are tightly packed together. The tighter the molecules, the harder will be the substance. Solids can hold their shape until an external energy is applied to it.

The atoms in a solid cannot move around. In liquids and gases, the atoms and molecules can move around, but in solids, they remain stuck. This is a physical characteristic of a solid.

Mixture of Rocks, Sand and Water

Solids can be made up of many things. They can contain one pure element or can be made up of various compounds. When there are a number of compounds that make up a solid, then it is called a **mixture**. Most **rocks** found on the earth are a **mixture of compounds**.

Concrete is a very useful man-made solid mixture that is used on a very large scale in the construction of buildings. Although when made, **concrete** is a liquid but when it is allowed to settle down, it becomes one of the hardest man-made solids.

Types of Solids

Crystalline Solids

Solids in which the atoms, ions and molecules are arranged in a definite pattern and in a three-dimensional order are called **crystals**. When a solid is made up of a pure element and forms slowly, it can become a crystal. Not all pure substances can form crystals because it is a very delicate process. A crystal is simply an organised group of atoms and molecules. Each crystal has different properties and shapes.

Carbon is an element which can exist in more than one crystalline form. *Graphite* is an example of a crystal of carbon. Graphite is soft and is used as a conductor of electricity, in pencils and in strengthening of steel. *Diamond*, another crystal of carbon is one of the hardest known substance. It is used as an industrial cutting tool and in jewellery.

Common Uses of Crystals

Precious Stones

Diamonds, rubies, sapphires and emeralds are all crystals that are used in jewellery as they are precious stones. They are highly valued and exist in a very limited quantity on the earth. In recent years, chemists have been able to make some of these crystals in laboratories with successful results.

Amorphous Solids

A Glass Window

In amorphous solids, particles are not arranged in any particular arrangement. Shapeless solids are called amorphous solids. Most solids are found in the amorphous form. Window glass, plastic materials and gels are amorphous solids.

A Plastic Plate

Properties and Uses of Solids

1. Physical Properties of Solids

Solids retain their shapes until or unless an external force is applied on them. They are hard to touch and cannot be compressed. Therefore, solids are used in places where there is a need to support something.

Solids are everywhere around us. The chair we sit on, cars and bikes in which we travel, mobile phone, computers all are solids. They are used for a variety of purposes.

Chair

Mobile

Computer

2. Mechanical Properties of Solids

A Spacecraft

Mechanical properties include elasticity, ductility, compressive strength, etc. Rubber is an elastic. Its shape can be changed when it is heated. Rubber is used in tyres, shoes and erasers, etc.

A Glass-top Stove

Glass-ceramics are used in counter-top cooking as they exhibit excellent mechanical properties. Polymers, ceramics and metal composite materials are used in aircraft and spacecraft exteriors.

3. Electrical Properties of Solids

Copper Electrical Wire

Electrical properties of solids include how well a substance conducts or resists electricity. **Semiconductors** act somewhere in between. Copper is a good **conductor** of electricity and is used to make electrical wires. Wood is a poor conductor of electricity or an **insulator** and therefore, it is recommended to use a wooden stool when working with electrical wires.

4. Thermal Properties of Solids

Utensils

Thermal properties of solids include how well a substance conducts heat. Some solids are good conductors of electricity but some are not. Iron, steel, aluminium, etc are good conductors and are therefore used in cooking utensils. Plastic and rubber are bad conductors of heat and are therefore used in making gloves to handle hot materials.

5. Magnetic Properties of Solids

A Magnet

As an electron is a charged particle, the circular motion of the electric charge causes the electron to act as a tiny electromagnet. *Iron, nickel and cobalt* are magnetic solids. Iron is used to make magnets which are then used for various purposes.

Quick Facts

- In solids, the atoms are fixed in location, but they constantly vibrate and vibrate faster with more heat. Thus, solids have a fixed shape.
- In liquids, the atoms are moving, bumping into each other but sticking to each other only momentarily. Thus, liquids take on the shape of their containers.
- In gases, the atoms are moving with high speed and frequently bump into each other without sticking. Therefore, gases also take the shape of their containers.
- Solids are of various types. Metals, their alloys, some non-metals, and ionic chemical compounds are crystalline in form. Some solids, e.g., chalk and clay, have no regular structure and are called amorphous. Substances, such as pitch and resin are called semisolids; these are actually very viscid liquids, but their flow or change of shape is so slow at ordinary temperatures as to be scarcely discernible by the human eye. Properties in which solids differ from one another include density, hardness, malleability, ductility, elasticity, brittleness, and tensile strength.

LIQUIDS

Liquid molecules are a little loosely packed. They can move around, and therefore liquids flow. Liquids have a fixed density but no fixed shape. A liquid can either be made up of a single substance or of two or more compounds. Liquids when made up of two or more compounds are called **solutions**.

A liquid generally takes the shape of its container. When you fill a glass with water, the water will first fill up the bottom and then rise up. It fills in the bottom first because of gravity.

Liquids are hard to compress. When we compress a substance, we take a certain amount of it and force it into a smaller space. To be able to get compressed, the atoms should have enough space between each other. Gases are very easily compressed as their atoms are far apart, while solids are the most difficult to compress because their atoms are tightly packed. In liquids too, the atoms are tightly packed but not like solids.

Liquid particles are bound firmly but not rigidly. When heat is applied, the molecules start moving faster and faster and when it reaches its boiling point, the liquids will change into a gas. In the opposite way, if the temperature is decreased, the molecules of a liquid will come closer together and become slow, this will change the liquid into a solid.

Uses of Liquids

Liquids have a lot of uses in our daily lives. Their uses depend upon their significant characteristics. Liquids are largely used as *lubricants, solvents*, and *coolants*.

Lubricant

Grease

A substance that is used to reduce friction when applied to a surface as a coating, particularly in moving parts of vehicles and machines is called a lubricant. *Oil* and *grease* are used in many machines as lubricants.

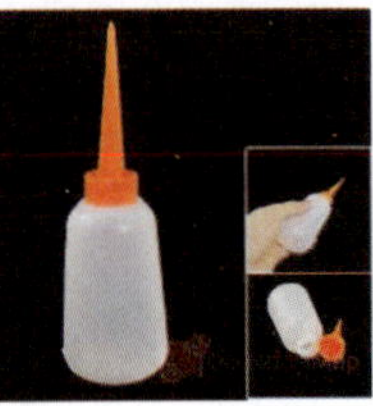

Machine Oil

Solvent

Adhesive

A solvent is a substance in which another substance is dissolved. Liquids are used as solvents to dissolve other liquids or solids in them. After dissolving another substance in a liquid, it becomes a solution. Solutions have a variety of uses. Some of the common solutions are adhesives, paints and sealants. Body fluids are also solutions that have *water* as their base.

Paint

Coolant

A coolant is an agent that produces cooling, generally a fluid that draws off heat. Liquids have a good thermal conductivity. Therefore *liquids* are more favourable to be used as coolants in machinery. In this process, either the liquid is made to travel through the heated part or the heated part is dipped into the liquid.

Radiator of a Car

Surface Tension

Have you ever tried to dive into a swimming pool and then fallen flat on the water instead? If yes, then you know about surface tension. It is because of surface tension that you get hurt and it feels as if the water has hit you back.

Drops of Water on a Leaf

Surface tension is the ability of a liquid to resist an external force. This happens because in a liquid, each molecule is pulling towards other molecules in all directions. But the molecules right at the surface are pulling in directions other than the upward direction. This creates a tension at the surface.

Viscosity

Some liquids flow freely, while some others don't. This depends on the viscosity of the liquid. In simple terms, viscosity is the thickness or the internal friction of a liquid. *Honey has a high viscosity* and therefore, it is thick, while *water has a low viscosity* and therefore, flows more freely.

A Drop of Honey Falls Slowly than Water

Quick Facts

- **Liquids can flow and their atoms are loosely packed. This does not mean that they are not strong. Water flowing in rivers can carve out rocks. In many places on the earth, rivers have carved out great valleys and canyons. The Grand Canyon is one such natural structure which has been carved out by the Colorado River.**

- Water settling on a leaf in the form of a drop is an example of surface tension. Water sticks weakly to the leaf and strongly to its own molecules and therefore, it forms a spherical shape or a drop.
- Roughly 70 percent of an adult's body is made up of water.
- At birth, water accounts for approximately 80 percent of an infant's body weight.
- A healthy person can drink about three gallons (48 cups) of water per day. However, drinking too much water too quickly can lead to water intoxication. Water intoxication occurs when water dilutes the sodium level in the bloodstream and causes an imbalance of water in the brain.
- While the daily recommended amount of water is eight cups per day, not all of this water must be consumed in the liquid form because nearly every food or drink item provides some water to the body.

Chapter - 15

GASES

Gases are all around us. *All the air around us is gas.* The atoms in a gas are very far apart and are full of energy. They keep bouncing around. *Gases neither have a definite shape nor a definite volume.*

Gases can fill a container of any size or shape. When you fill a balloon with a gas, it spreads to the whole of the balloon. If we fill a balloon with a liquid then the liquids always settles at the bottom first.

A Balloon Filled with Air

Vapour and gas are the same thing. Although the term vapour is generally used for gases that are usually found as liquids. Gases like carbon dioxide and nitrogen are found in the gaseous state at room temperature therefore they will not be called vapours. When water turns into a gas, it is called water vapour.

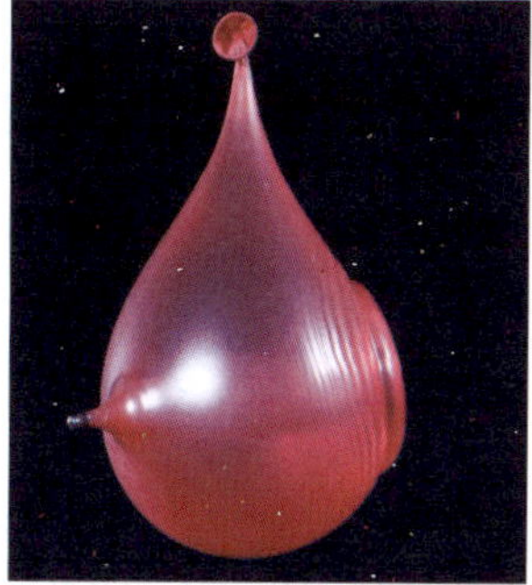

A Balloon Half Filled with Air

The atoms and molecules in gases are spread out as much as they can be. Gases have a lot of energy in them. They can float about and get into a tiny amount of space.

Gases can be compressed with little pressure. For example, compressed air is in a spray bottle and it gets released when we press the bottle. Also when we open soft drink cans we can hear the gas escaping from it, this is also the gas compressed in the can.

Deodorant Bottle

A pure gas can be made up of individual atoms or molecules made up of one type of atoms like neon or compound molecules made from a variety of atoms like car dioxide. A gas mixture can contain a variety of different gas atoms like air.

A Soft Drink Can

The air we breathe contains 78% nitrogen, 21% oxygen, 1% argon, .03% carbon dioxide and small measures of other gases.

Gases are generally invisible to the eye. You can feel the presence of a gas sometimes by its smell, or the sound or if it has a particular colour.

Physical Characteristics of Gases

Density and Viscosity

Compared to liquids and solids, gases have a very low density and viscosity. They flow easily and take up space inside the container they are. The atoms spread out and cover the whole container.

Pressure

The term, pressure in gases is referred to the amount of force the gas exerts on the surface area of a container. Gas pressure is measured in **Pascal**.

Temperature

The temperature of a gas can be determined by us by simply feeling if one gas is hotter than the other. In a hot gas, the molecules move faster than the molecules in a cold gas. The temperature is more because the molecules in a hotter gas move faster.

Atmospheric Pressure

A Barometer

The atmosphere of the earth is made up of many gases. All these gases exert a pressure on everything on the earth's surface. This pressure is called the atmospheric pressure. In the early 17th century, **Evangelista Torricelli** invented a **barometer** to measure the pressure that our atmosphere exerts on us. Torricelli's invention contradicted the belief of people that air is weightless.

Evangelista Torricelli

Quick Facts

- **The ozone layer in the earth's atmosphere protects the earth from the sun's harmful Ultraviolet rays. Ozone has three oxygen atoms bound together. The Ozone layer is a part of the Stratosphere and it is not very thick. The Ozone layer is thicker near the equator and thinner near the poles.**
- **It has been observed that the ozone layer is depleting. Since it protects the earth from harmful UV rays that can cause skin cancer, the ozone layer depletion is a cause for concern. The depletion has been greatest at high altitudes and mostly notable in Antarctica during winter.**

- The air we breathe on earth is made up of different gases. It contains around 78% nitrogen, 21% oxygen, 1% argon and a small amount of other gases.
- Natural gas contains mostly methane. It is used as a fuel to generate electricity and is common in homes, where it can be used for heating, cooking and other purposes.
- The gas pressure is measured in Pascal.
- The helium balloons you get at parties and carnivals float because helium is lighter than the air surrounding it.
- Noble gases are a group of chemical elements that are very stable under normal conditions. Naturally occurring noble gases include Helium, Neon, Argon, Krypton, Xenon and Radon.

Exercises

I. Answer the following questions.

1. What is matter and what are the four main types of matter that exist on the earth? Describe briefly.
2. What are the different properties based on which materials can be classified? Explain them briefly.
3. Explain the following terms briefly with one example each. Melting, Freezing, Evaporation and Condensation.
4. What is an atom and what is it made of? Explain with the help of a diagram.
5. What is chemical bonding and what are the two different types of chemical bonds?
6. Define Mass, Volume and Density. How are they measured? Explain their relationship with the help of a formula.
7. What is a molecule? Explain the structure of a water molecule and the bond formed between the atoms of a water molecule.
8. What are elements and how are they arranged in a periodic table?
9. What are metals and non-metals? Explain with two of their properties and examples.
10. What do you understand by the physical and chemical properties of elements? Explain with the help of an example.

II. Fill in the blanks with suitable words.

1. When different elements bond together through a chemical reaction, they form __________.
2. __________ are formed when elements are mixed together and no bonding takes place.
3. Examples of compounds are __________ and __________.
4. To get pure iron, elements, such as iron and oxygen have to be separated and this is done in a __________.
5. The two different types of compounds are: __________ and __________.
6. When a mixture is formed, no energy is either __________ or __________.
7. In a sugar-water solution, sugar is called the _______ and water is called the _______.
8. A __________ is a mixture of two substances which do not dissolve completely.
9. __________ of iron takes a long time, while cooking creates chemical reactions in minutes.
10. A __________ change may change the size, shape or colour of a substance, but does not change its composition.

III. Match the two columns correctly.

A	B
1. A reversible chemical change is	with bases to form salt and water.
2. A pH scale is used to measure	sulphur dioxide and nitrogen dioxide from polluting clouds.

3. Acids taste sour and they react	how acidic or basic a solution is.
4. An Acid Rain is the combination of	because their molecules are tightly packed together.
5. Solids are mostly hard	turning water into hydrogen and oxygen.

IV. Multiple Choice Questions (MCQs)

1. A solid in which the atoms, ions and molecules are arranged in a definite pattern and in a three-dimensional order is called ____________.

   a. Crystals b. Stones

   c. Semi-solids d. Metals

2. A liquid generally takes the shape of its ____________.

   a. Molecules b. Container

   c. Atoms d. Volume

3. Thermal properties of solids include how well a substance ____________.

   a. Conducts Electricity b. Conducts Force

   c. Conducts Heat d. None of these

4. Window glass, plastic materials and gels are examples of ____________.

   a. Amorphous liquids b. Transparent solids

   c. Amorphous solids d. None of these

5. Litmus is a substance obtained from lichens, which is a/an ____________.

   a. Algae b. Fungi

   c. Bacteria d. Virus

6. Surface tension is the ability of a liquid to resist an ____________.

   a. External force

   b. Internal force

   c. Both Internal & External force

   d. None of these

7. The ozone layer in the earth's atmosphere protects the earth from the sun's harmful ____________.

   a. Ultraviolet rays b. Infrared rays

   c. Ultrasonic rays d. Cosmic rays

8. Acids change litmus paper from blue to

   a. Orange b. Green

   c. Red e. Yellow

Glossary

Electromagnetic Radiation: Radiation originating from visible light, radio waves, x-rays

Compressible: To press together, or to cause to become a solid mass

Combine: Join together

Definite: Particular shape, volume

Rigid: Inflexible, Firm, Fixed

Container: Vessel

Atmosphere: Environment

Ionizing: To separate or change into ions

Conductive: Denoting or having the property of conduction

Properties: Features

Fluorescent: Strikingly bright

Lightning: A brilliant shark or discharge of light during thunderstorm

Condensate: A substance formed by condensation

Super-unexcited: Super-inactive

Blob: A globule of liquid, bubble

Element: Substance, component

Vacuum: A space entirely devoid of matter

Plasma: A highly ionized gas containing an equal number of positive ions and electrons

Pressure: The exertion of force upon a surface by an object, fluid

Temperature: A measure of warmth or coldness of an object of a living body

Density: The state or quality of being dense, or mass per unit volume

Vapour: Particles of moisture or other substances suspended in air, substance in a gaseous state

Brittle: Hard, rough, rigid

Transparent: Allowing the passage of light

Freezing: Chilled, to become hardened into a solid

Boiling: Steaming or reaching the boiling point

Melting: To become a liquid

Flexibility: Capable of being bent, can easily undergo change

Rigidity: Stiff or inflexible

Evaporation: The process of changing a liquid into gas or vapour

Galaxy: A large system of stars held together by mutual gravitation

Microscope: An optical instrument having a magnifying lens

Periodic Table: A table of elements containing metals and non-metals

Atom Bomb: A type of bomb in which energy is provided by nuclear fission

CHILDREN'S ENCYCLOPEDIA

THE WORLD OF KNOWLEDGE

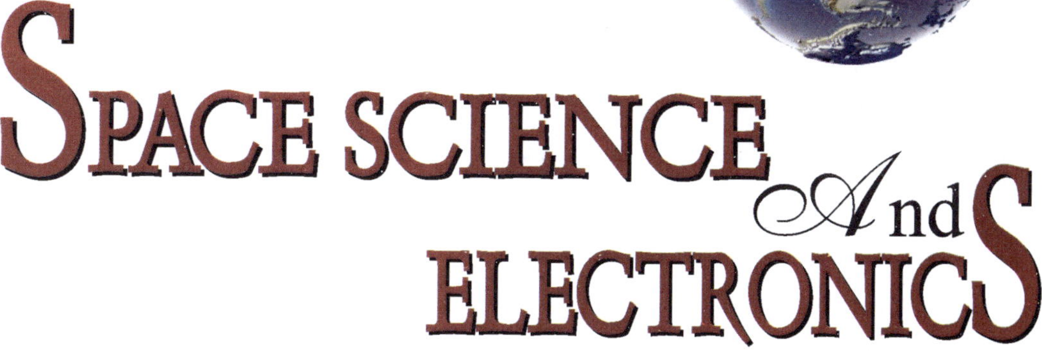

by

Manasvi Vohra

Published by:

Head Office
F-2/16, Ansari Road, Daryaganj,
New Delhi-110002 ☎ 23240026, 27, 28
✉ info@vspublishers.com
www.vspublishers.com

Regional Office
5-1-707/1, Brij Bhawan (Beside Central
Bank of India Lane) Bank Street, Koti,
Hyderabad - 500 095 ☎ 040-24737290
✉ vspublishershyd@gmail.com

Online Brandstore: amazon.in/vspublishers

Buy Books Online: amazon • Flipkart | **Follow us on:**   

ISBN 978-93-505703-8-8

New Edition

Cataloging in Publication Data--DK
Courtesy: D.K. Agencies (P) Ltd. <docinfo@dkagencies.com>

Vohra, Manasvi, author.
Space science and electronics / Manasvi Vohra.
pages cm. -- (Children's encyclopedia : the world of knowledge)
ISBN 9789350570388

1. Space sciences--Encyclopedias, Juvenile. 2. Electronics--Encyclopedias, Juvenile. I. Title. II. Series: Children's encyclopedia : the world of knowledge.

LCC QB500.22.V64 2024 | DDC 550.503 23

Printed at : Param Offsetters, Okhla, New Delhi–110020